Scott
Christmas 2007!
Enjoy the great story
of Miki whose influence
on surfing & the making
of surfing as a cult will
last & last. Love Kiki + Sue

Surfing hedonist who became a hero to a generation of beach bums, before turning his back on the waves Mickey Dora was everything that a surfer ought to be: he was tanned, he was good-looking, and he was trouble. West Coast archetype and antihero, he became the incarnation of surfing for the postwar generation. Technically, he was an innovator whose effortless grace and balletic suppleness (which gave him his nickname, "Da Cat") set new standards.

But he was above all the siren voice of a nonconformist surfing lifestyle, making a career out of never holding down a serious job and injecting the brash hedonism of the beach into the culture at large. Even among surfers, Dora was notorious. Indeed, he was so much a rebel that he rebelled, in the end, against surfing.

Born in Budapest in 1934, Miklos Sandor Dora moved to California as a child, and attended Hollywood High School unless the surf was up. He learnt the art of boardriding at San Onofre from his stepfather, Gard Chapin, in the 1940s, and by the Fifties he was one of the leading lights of Malibu, where he drew new lines across the long lazy point-break waves on his Quigg pintail.

With the publication of Frederick Kohner's 1957 book *Gidget* (based on his daughter's adventures at Malibu) and the subsequent epidemic of naive Hollywood romances--notably *Bikini Beach*, *How to Stuff a Wild Bikini* and *For Those who Think Young*-- which he played bit-parts, Dora was consecrated as the profane evangelist of a youthful counterculture.

He performed as a stunt double in *Ride the Wild Surf* (1963), which was distinguished not only by songs from Jan and Dean and Brian Wilson of Beach Boys fame, but by some serious 20ft-plus surf at Waimea Bay on the North Shore of Hawaii.

But if he had the ability and courage to surf big waves, he lacked the desire, and specialized instead in maximizing the style factor in the mannered manoeuvres of small-wave riding. His technique may have been the origin of the term "laid-back", as he typically leant backwards on his board slightly bent at the knee. "Mickey had a tremendous influence on us as surfers," said John Milius, a friend of Dora's and director of *Big Wednesday*, the classic elegy of the West Coast Utopia. "Everybody tried to surf like him and have his grace and his style and cool."

It was a brief golden age that was destroyed by its own popularity. "I grew up under this wonderful freedom," Dora said, "but it went so quickly." A soul-surfer at heart, Dora became increasingly hostile to the professional and commercial evolution of the sport. Although intensely competitive, he denounced competitions, pulling down his trunks to moon at the judges at the 1967 Malibu Invitational.

Dora was a Kerouac in shorts, the soulmate of Jack Nicholson in *One Flew Over the Cuckoo's Nest*: a subversive, restless wildman. He was a joker who fired off army flares on the pier at Malibu and played tennis in a trenchcoat. With an essentially religious mentality,

2

he was haunted by a deep sense of paradise lost, and looked forward to some catastrophic apocalypse restoring the original purity. Meanwhile, he continued to ride his own miniature version of the Ark, on which only he would be saved.

The more mainstream surfing became, the more he felt marginal and alienated. He grew up when barely a handful of people would be found out on the break, so he hated crowds, and was often ill-tempered and ungenerous towards fellow surfers, even — perhaps especially — to those who liked and admired him. He believed he had a divine right to every wave at Malibu, and took to painting swastikas on his board.

"I remember riding this one wave and someone pushing me off my board from behind, screaming, 'Go home you little creep'," recalled the curator of the Santa Barbara Surfing Museum, Jim O'Mahoney. It was Dora. "As a little kid, it was like getting yanked from your board by God. It was a badge of honour."

There used to be a quasi- monastic creed among surfers that one had to choose between women and waves: you couldn't have both. Dora chose waves. When he took off from California in the early Seventies, some said that it was the endless quest for the perfect wave, though others said that it was not unconnected to his habit of passing bad cheques. Either way, he was arrested by the FBI in 1981 for having fled the country in violation of parole.

While in prison he was sentenced to a further six months for using a stolen credit card on a two-year spending spree through Europe and Asia. Maybe this was a spirited protest against capitalism, or perhaps it was simply that Dora felt the world owed him a living for being Mickey Dora. In any case, his spell in jail only enhanced the legend in the morally inverted realm of surfing.

Dora attained mythic status long before his death. After his departure, "Dora lives" was painted on the wall at Malibu, and over the next three decades there were reported sightings of him as far apart as South Africa, New Zealand and Chile.

He was rumoured to have settled for a while in Guethary, on the Atlantic coast of southwest France, but even in the 1990s one film-maker could still produce an enigmatic documentary called *In Search of Da Cat*. He was more symbol than surfer, and his legacy is his attitude.

Only when Dora discovered, in July 2001, that he was suffering from pancreatic cancer did he give up his exile and return to his father's home in Montecito, California.

Mickey Dora, surfer, was born in Budapest on August 11, 1934. He died on January 3, 2002, aged 67.

Dora Lives   The Authorized Story of Miki Dora

C.R.Stecyk III and Drew Kampion

T. Adler Books, Santa Barbara

Writing about Mickey Dora can be a fool's game – surf journalist quicksand. It's hard not to lapse into his trap, especially if you've spent any time with him and had him run you through his maize like a rat in a labyrinth. The experience, however brief, might give you the impression that you've earned some justification for delving into him. That would be unlikely. Dora has been sliced and diced relentlessly, yet he remains an enigma, bigger in life than in death, yet still confounding. His lingering aura is like a persistent nag, demanding that we attempt to decode it. In the process we end up Rorschaching ourselves more than he, caught in a Dora quagmire, as exposed and naked as truth. Dora would be amused.

Tom Adler, the maker of this book, traveled to visit Dora in France when Mickey was announced to be critically ill but still robust. As Mickey faded towards the end and came to Santa Barbara, California, to be with his father, Adler had already begun gathering for this book, which began as collaboration between the two. Mickey felt an urgency to leave a tangible legacy and Adler's

prior photo book on Dr. Don James appealed greatly to him. With Mickey's blessing, Adler had set to work sleuthing for images that would elucidate Dora in surprising and wonderful ways. Tom also enlisted two storied wordsmiths for their contributions, Drew Kampion and Craig Stecyk. Each had personal views of Mickey. Drew's began from a distance, as an aspiring journalist whose first submitted freelance writing, a short homage on Dora at Malibu, was rejected by *Surfer* founder John Severson. Kampion soon after became editor of *Surfer* and was at the helm during its finest moments in the late 1960s. In that capacity he was to observe Dora's full range of antics, including jousts of gamesmanship with Severson, from close range. During that same time Craig Stecyk and Mickey became acquaintances at Malibu. A mutual intelligence, diversity of interests, and cynical outlook may have created the affinity. Mickey took a liking to young Craig, and they stayed in touch thereafter. It seemed that Dora trusted Stecyk as much as he could anyone. Perhaps it was because, unlike others who pressed in close to suck up, Craig wanted nothing from him. Near the end, it was he who Mickey trusted to record hours of his rambling reminisces. As the body of material took shape, Adler began adapting it into that which you now hold in your hands. Like anything involving Mickey, it entailed a twisted journey. Tom's gift is in his vision and his eye. He sees the subtle potential and poignancy in images that most would miss. His graphic packaging is spare, letting the content be the star. The resultant presentation becomes a statement for both the subject and himself.

At the time I wrote these thoughts I had not yet seen what this book had become. I anticipate that more than any set of words could accomplish, the images within define Mickey Dora more deftly and innately than I have ever thought possible of myself. For the committed surfer, Dora's reality is worth revisiting, if even for a moment. Mickey lived it full time. It was his private heaven and his hell. This book is a small shrine of sorts, to both places.

Steve Pezman, San Clemente, California

This book is a blend of voices. Unattributed text is by Drew Kampion. CRS *denotes text authored by C.R.Stecyk III.* MSD *denotes comments by Miki S. Dora (audio taped or otherwise).*

Misdirection is the currency of the conjurer. Our friend is gone. Miklos Sandor Dora, aka Mickey Chapin, Michael Chapin Dora, Dickie Mora … and those are only his government names. When you consider some of his other monikers, like Da Cat, the Tennis Shoe Kid, Malibu Mickey, MSD XXV, King 'Bu, the Fiasco Kid, and the Black Knight, it starts to get genuinely bewildering. Some call him a fraud, a forger, a liar, a thief, and a luckless soldier of misfortune. Some call him the greatest surfer that ever lived, a poet, a philosopher, an artist, and the progenitor of integrated urbane beach culture. Miki himself would deny all of the above citing obscure statutes of Roman Imperial law, which absolved victims of misidentification from any complicity in these matters. – CRS

He surfed like a god, and that's all we knew of him – that and his reputation and maybe a few encounters with him on the beach and in the water at Malibu. His disdain, his imperial presence, his ownership of everything great and good (which was that beach and those waves), his presence at his spot relegated everyone and everything else to mere second fiddle. He walked the beach with a contemptuous authority, with a peculiar cant and shuffling cadence that was uniquely his. His very disregard made the rest of us seem common and dull, and somehow subjugated. We thought he'd always been there, as constant and iconic as the waves themselves. We imagined him as we thought he was.

He surfed like a god … with a deific ease and effortless poise, an air of intricate calculation. One felt concentrated awareness and sensed a subtle grandeur. When he fell, if it was ugly, we were embarrassed for him. We hated to see him miscalculate or screw up; it subtracted from the trance of cool awe he commanded, momentarily flattening the apex of our very sport's achievement … so much did he define and personify it for us, we who were the young surfers of Malibu in the early 1960s.

He surfed, too, with an instinctive wit, a Hollywood air, a commanding if self-conscious presence. He brought theatre and a sense of cinema to the sand. He surfed seriously but with an easy grin, was mean as an assassin, but seemed also sensitive and hurt by it all – the ending of his era and all of that – the loss of Malibu to the clutter of the mindless masses that brimmed over from the San Fernando Valley and crowded his perfect waves with their inane stupidity and crass ignorance.

He loathed us all, and for good reason – we were intruding, and there was no denying it. He loathed himself for compromising – for turning tricks for the Hollywood fat cats pimping his California surf dream to sequential cultural waves of hypnotized fans and pretenders. He hated himself for ratting on the scene and settling for the quick buck … hated his new life and grappled with the sell-out before bowing out and bending over with a deft drop of his baggies, mooning the surf-contest judges on his last wave out of town.

Flaunting his disheveled grace, he was surfing's Brando (who he admired and from whom he drew and assimilated pregnant physical attitudes), and he spoke in the same shuffling way he walked, with a mumbling but smooth cadence. He was our Elvis, our Belmondo. There was no one else that filled the bill, no one else whose insouciant posture and critical mindset could simultaneously focus, represent, and express both the emergent beach culture's physical and symbolic importance … no one else to articulate the fundamental gestures of the sociopathic manifesto of a coalescing youth consciousness.

Whatever it took, Dora broke down the old with a sneer. A pragmatic iconoclast with a sufficiently suppressed conscience to shrug off any collateral damage, he was not prone to entertain fools, unless they were useful to his immediate purposes. Thus he was reviled, too, in a persistent chorus of accusation and revelation – that he was crazy, a kleptomaniac and misogynist, conman and fraud, a petty (and not so petty) thief. Oh yes, and that, actually, he couldn't really surf … certainly not large waves.

Some knew a different truth, knew that it was all about style and, by extrapolation, that it was about

Miki and mother. 1936. Courtesy Family of M.S. Dora

Cadet M. S. Dora. St. John's Military Academy, 1944. Courtesy Family of M.S. Dora

art, and about living artfully and being artful. Some saw that Dora's was a guerrilla stance in the midst of the socially-reorganizing 1950s. Clearly, he felt foreign and estranged on his own turf, even as he tried hard to hold back the changes that had been set in motion on the far side of the coastal mountains. He fought to keep the sands free and unfettered, defied the conservative lifeguard mindset, endeavoring to keep the coast wild, to maintain and even cultivate its manifest outlaw badland designation.

Inevitably all he held dear and perfect would bleed out through his grasping fingers. Even as he watched, it all disappeared. No matter how strongly he held onto the present, everything worth anything soon trailed away behind him into the past, and the only way to find it again was to go some place where that hadn't already happened.

> My own father taught me a gracious manner of living, while my stepfather showed me how to survive when confronted with adversity. Which was the better? Which was the worse? One father showed how to atone for indiscretions and the other demonstrated how to commit them. I was able to live to tell the tale because of the imbalance inspired by both. – MSD

He was born in Budapest, but the family came almost immediately to Los Angeles, where Ramona Stanclif had lived before she met her Royal Cavalry officer, Miklos Kornel Dora. They arrived in January of 1935, in time for the opening of the new Griffith Observatory and Amelia Earhart Putnam's sendoff on her historic solo flight to Mexico City. Miklos intended to make a living marketing Hungarian wines, while the city was trying to find a way to stem the flow of unemployed Los Angeles-bound hitchhikers.

At the beginning, everything must have seemed perfect – the ocean, the golden hills, the blowing trees, flowers forever opening, all the sweet sounds and plein-air feasts of perfect days in Southern California. But then came the contradictions, force fed by the sheer circumstances of existence, by the simple challenges of people and things. His mother's attention was drawn elsewhere; although she loved him

First paddle out at San Onofre, Early Forties. Courtesy Family of M.S. Dora

Stepfather Gard Chapin. Bluff Cove, 1936. Photo Don James

Miklos and Miki, 1943. Courtesy Family of M.S. Dora

San Onofre Jam Session, 1948. Photo Joe Quigg

dearly, she was easily distracted from the duties of motherhood. She might forget him altogether for quite some time. As it so often does, life began to come apart for Miki. In the end, as the beam of attraction drew her from her family and into the outrageous world of a man by the name of Gardner Chapin, things changed utterly for the six-year-old kid, who suddenly found himself enrolled in St. John's Military Academy, a Catholic school which had been the elementary alma mater of Gregory Peck and Lash LaRue.

A couple of summers before, he had been introduced to the ocean and surfing by his father in the small waves of Paddleboard Cove on the north side of Palos Verdes. But his brief exposure to the California coastal idyll was short-lived, as the divorce of Miklos and Ramona ripped away his past entire and swept in a new, charismatic, and powerful stepfather, one Gard Chapin, a legend of insult and aggravation and prowess, too – a hard case with a red-necked white man's prejudices.

The boy's sensitive and artistic nature found no comfort in the rigid rules and regimentation of institutional education, no warmth at all in his subsequent enrollment at St. Victor's Catholic school. With his father estranged on a different strata of Los Angeles society, the boy was trapped in an oscillation between negative poles … but with intermittent shards of clarity. Those transcendent times of freedom were most often experienced on summertime visits to a remote beach on the northern fringes of San Diego County and a place called San Onofre. Ironically, this was common turf for both the father and the stepfather.

Miklos described the early days at Sano in the most elegiac terms – the warm, remote beach, the nights spent in that pre-World War II wilderness. He loved the solitude, the ocean, and was content to slide a few modest waves on his hollow "kook box." Chapin, on the other hand, was already developing a reputation as one of the best surfers on the coast, and his brash, cocked personality had already established him with an identity in the nascent California beach culture. Contemporaries of Chapin almost unanimously recall his mean streak, especially if he'd been drinking. He is credited with inventing the deep drop-knee turn, a stylistic maneuver that was pivotal in the evolution of surfing performance beyond the conservative approach of the era.

Dora's involvement with wave riding began when his birth father first took him out at Paddleboard Cove in 1938. His interest in the activity intensified when his mother Ramona married Gardner Chapin, a leading figure in the emergent sport. Chapin was renowned for his unique ability to maneuver his heavy plank surfboards and simultaneously perform dazzlingly intricate footwork. Young Dora was exposed to virtually all of the principal proponents and locations of mainland surfing through Chapin. He also served an informal apprenticeship in Gard's woodshop, where he built surfboards alongside his stepfather and Bob Simmons. The latter is the single most recognized innovator of modern-type surfboard design. Gardner Chapin's expertise in early composite and laminated wood constructions allowed him to interact with a network of aircraft, watercraft, and architectural engineers, including such notables as the Vultee brothers, Preston "Pete" Petersen, Tom Blake, Howard Hughes, and Charles and Ray Eames. As an apprentice surfboard constructor, Miki Dora had enviable access to both advanced theory and rare and at times classified exotic materials and methodologies. – CRS

About the time he took up with Ramona, Chapin began to play a critical role in the history of surfing. A carpenter and handyman, he'd fallen off a ladder, broken a leg, and was in the hospital where he overheard some nearby drama: a young man, childhood cancer survivor, had been critically injured in a bicycle accident – fractured skull, broken leg, smashed left elbow. The head and leg had healed, but the arm was now wired in a loosely extended position, and the doctors were saying that unless he found some way to exercise the limb, it might have to be amputated. Chapin later slipped in and told the young man about surfing – stoked him on wave-riding and suggested that paddling a surfboard would be perfect physical therapy.

Miki. San Onofre. 1950. Courtesy Family of M.S. Dora. Photographer unknown

The injured man was Bob Simmons, a brilliant mathematician with a scholarship at Cal Tech and as edgy a personality as Chapin's. Under Gard's tutelage Simmons acquired a hollow Tom Blake paddleboard and began a diligent recovery effort. By wartime, Simmons was so surf-stoked he'd walk out on his job at Douglas Aircraft whenever the waves were up. Chapin had a door-making business in his garage, and it was nicely set up for building surfboards as well. It was there in the late 1940s that Simmons pulled together his hydrodynamic theories and interpreted them with newly discovered composite materials to create the first foam and fiberglass surfboards, and this was a big thing in the history of surfing.

The situation was opportune for young Miki to absorb the lessons of these two protean masters — from surfboard construction to an understanding of the world of waves, from beach culture, such as it was, to personal style. Importantly, what Simmons possessed in technical ability, he lacked in social tolerance. A restless loner, he shared Chapin's distaste for inept intruders who ignored the unwritten cardinal rule of surfing: You don't take off on a wave someone else is already riding.

Gard Chapin was a relentless individualist with whom no holds were barred and all the moves were unconventional. Once, in the middle of the night, he came into my bedroom and woke me up.
"Hey kid, you've got to come with me to see something." Then he dragged me down to Hollywood Boulevard. "Look around … what do you see that's wrong here?"
Then he opened the trunk on his car and took out a sledgehammer and walked me over to the curb.
"Miki, these bastards want to control everything. Now they want to make us pay money to park on the street."
Chapin then smashed the head off every brand new parking meter that the city had just installed. It was the first day they had been put out, and he creamed every one of them for several blocks. His anger and the point of it were something that you could never forget seeing. When he was finished he suddenly became very calm, and he climbed up the sign pole on the corner.

"Here's a souvenir."

He handed me the street sign from Hollywood and Vine. I kept it for years until it was lost when they auctioned off all my stuff in Gisborne, New Zealand. – MSD

For much of his youth (from 1942 until through high school), Miki lived with his father's mother. Madam Nadina DeSanctis had come to Los Angeles from Vienna in 1937, the year Miklos opened his "Little Hungary" restaurant on Sunset Boulevard. She was a woman of high culture, a revered concert pianist and an excellent voice coach, and her classically-appointed West Hollywood home was the essence of all things refined and proper. This was in stark contrast to the domicile of Ramona and Gard, who were living in a converted garage in the San Fernando Valley. Nonetheless, when Miklos abruptly moved to Argentina in 1948 to adventure in the shrimp business, it was Gard who was there to haul Miki down to San Onofre to surf, and on more than one occasion forget to bring him home.

More or less adrift throughout his years of minimal participation at Hollywood High, Miki followed his interests and instincts, exploring the world that was available, wandering fertile Southern California in post-War boom times, exploring the culture, the art, the music. He studied magic tricks and automobiles and honed his gift for humor and discourse. Inspired by his surfboard-building experiences with Chapin and Simmons, he fashioned a surfboard in Madam's garage using salvage balsa from a Navy gunnery target, then bored out the hull and filled it with ping-pong balls (probably for lightness and buoyancy) and, finally, meticulously laminated its fiberglass exterior. That it came apart on the rocks at Rincon, scattering ping-pong balls across the beach, is not the point.

Surfboards were improving; balsa was coming in, so the boards were much lighter than they had been, and the fiberglass-and-resin lamination process had improved. It was getting easier to surf. Up at Malibu, a few women were picking up the sport, and some kids. Even so, in the summer of 1950, it was

Malibu. Summer, 1951. Photo Joe Quigg

mostly just Mickey Dora and Terry Tracey, the only kids hanging out and surfing down at "Old 'Nofre," where the surfers were mostly older World War II vets and their girlfriends. Naturally enough, the scene reflected the general ethos of a predominantly male sporting activity with its attendant hierarchy and license. The atmosphere was right to elicit a conspiratorial response from the young lads, a shared sense of imagination, opportunism, and mischief.

Perhaps the greatest creation of an artist is the persona of the artist himself. You can see the artist as "a sensitive" … or as a human being that has failed at being completely hypnotized like the rest of the population. The artist is painfully (and perhaps not unconsciously) aware of this – aware of his or her objective isolation, as opposed to the subjective isolation of the general, so-called "normal" population, which the artist perceives as not unlike the walking dead. There's an ethic in surf culture that opposes the overly structured life. That refuses to comply with insistence. That resists temptation. Of a sort.

Take one unusually bright, perceptive, and sensitive child, run him through military school, archetypal opposing fathers, sensual and nurturing females, the influence of a cultured grandmother (not to mention a Simmons) and turn him loose in Southern California in the 1950s and, oh yeah, have him discover that the highest expression of his artistic drive is surfing on perfect Malibu waves. And imagination! Imagination might rate highest of all as an expression of his artistic drive.

Miki's natural course, the logical path for his mercurial and aesthetic temperament, was the Gypsy life – resisting, challenging, debunking, undermining, outfoxing – using the tools of cynicism and high comedy in a truly iconoclastic revel of a personality. Someone you might well describe as incorrigible, a sociopath, or maybe a hedonist. Your perspective depended on where you stood with Miki – whether he toyed with you, stole from you, lied to you, or opened up to you made all the difference, naturally.

Lavishly if erratically loved and praised by his mother, given loving structure by the grandmother, Dora's sense of self was no doubt great, but with an accompanying (and warranted) feeling of exposure.

He was charismatic. Does such a situation add ballast to the keel of one's ego? Does it serve as a crash course in human dynamics? What does a Gypsy spirit do with all of this?

Just as Brando had answered the sheriff's daughter's question, "What are you rebelling against?" with "What have you got?" so Dora would be a pathfinder in a new field of relationship that would connect the beat generation with the beach generation. He would bring his particular artistic vocabulary to the act of riding a wave; where others had been artful, he would bring the full palette of the artist's sensibility to his relationship – not only with waves, with the way he surfed, and why he surfed.

Five hundred million years ago Southern California was submerged under the ocean. Los Angeles' best neighborhoods were reefs. Palos Verdes, Malibu, Bunker Hill, Beverly Hills were only soggy and sunken. L.A.'s city hall is built on seashells, the library rests on sand, and the art museum floats upon pits of La Brea mastodon tar. I've been studying the geological and storm records, and they indicate that the Pacific coast has been in a 200-year-long lull for storms. The reefs and points are all set up to hold much bigger waves. It is only a matter of time until the sea gods come and reclaim their domain. All of the development will be washed away by the incoming tide of nature's revenge. – MSD

In 1952, he flew south to visit his father, stopped over in Haiti to visit Miklos' second wife Lorraine and Pauline, then continued on to Argentina, where Miklos was doing business out of Mar Del Plata, which would become ground zero for Argentine surfing 25 years later. On the way home to California, Miki surfed near Santiago, Chile, possibly the first one ever to do so; he then flew on to Peru, where he surfed at a spot called Miraflores with members of the Club Waikiki, founded by Carlos Dogny ten years before.

He was 18 years old and needed to make it back to register with the Selective Service, which he did, and was rejected for his chronic asthma. After that, there was nothing stopping him. He considered Santa Monica City College, checked out the courses, visualized his future more than a little, and then he went to

Miki and half-sister Pauline. Haiti, 1952. Courtesy Family of M.S.Dora

the beach, to the Malibu.

Back in 1805, the Spanish governor had granted this coastal land to a former soldier, Jose Tapia, who named his new 13,000-acre coastal spread Rancho Topanga Malibu Sequit. Frederick Hastings Rindge and May Knight Rindge became the last owners of the Rancho Malibu Spanish grant in the late 1800s, and after Frederick's death in 1905, his wife famously and furiously fought to keep it sacrosanct. Rindge spent her considerable fortune defending the Malibu against intrusions by the Southern Pacific Railroad, the State, and neighboring homesteaders, but by the mid-1920s she was forced to lease then sell small parcels of beachfront property north of the mouth of Malibu Creek. Since the first lots were offered to movie celebrities (Ronald Coleman among them), the strand became known as the Malibu Movie Colony. May ultimately failed to keep the world out of her rancho; the Roosevelt Highway (now Pacific Coast Highway) was opened between Santa Monica and Oxnard in June of 1929, and the beach between the pier and the mouth of the creek opened to the public.

In the post-war 1940s and '50s, the relatively remote Malibu coast remained a borderland frontier with considerable ecological integrity – an idyllic stretch of points and coves that served as a refuge and retreat not only for celebrities but for others looking to distance themselves from the increasing frenzy just a few miles away. The public beach north of the Malibu pier became the focus; here a jutting cobblestone point caught the swells pulsing north from summer chubascos off Mexico and bent them into silky-smooth waves that wrapped along the broad, sandy beach towards the pier – perfect surf for the lightweight, maneuverable balsa boards.

Chapin and Simmons rode the Malibu in those days, along with the great Pete Peterson, Matt Kivlin, Joe Quigg, Dave Rochlen, Kit Horn, Dale Velzy, and a dozen or so others, including pioneer female surfer Mary Ann Hawkins. As with San Onofre, when Miki started surfing Malibu regularly, there were few other young riders in the lineup. Finally, everything once again made sense in his life – at least while he was

Schazamm board, 1962. Courtesy family of M. S. Dora. Photographer unknown

sliding across the face of one of those Malibu curls. The utter beauty of the place and the wave was overwhelming, and he reveled in it.

With unprecedented enthusiasm and concentration, Miki devoted himself to surfing Malibu, and Chapin took notice of his stepson's promise – he looked so at home on a board, so in his element. Joe Quigg had been influenced by Gard and Simmons, but he was now on his own and experimenting with elegant balsa pintails designed for easier rail-to-rail transitions. Chapin bought Joe's Malibu "easy rider" for Miki. Slightly wider (21") and friendlier than the other "Rincon" speed models, it was Quigg's fifth pintail. Dora accounted it his first great surfboard. It challenged his abilities, and his surfing advanced rapidly to keep pace with the board. Mickey Chapin was getting a reputation as a hot new kid at Malibu. He was feeling like he was in the sweet spot, slotted into the wave of his life.

Equipment is everything in surfing, or just about. With the new balsa boards, the static surfing stances and straight-line surfing of the past began to give way to speedy turns and an era of tricks, stunts, and show-off maneuvers.

As word got out about the new boards – that the days of 75-pound redwoods and surfboards made by ladder companies were gone and that "Malibu chips" were the thing – other young kids began showing up at the point. Lance Carson, Mickey Muñoz, Kemp Aaberg, Dewey Weber, Bob Cooper, Mike Doyle, Jim Fisher, Johnny Fain, Tom Morey, and Robert Patterson joined Mickey and Tracey, who was soon dubbed "Tubesteak," as a club-like sense community began to jell and the regulars began to assume nicknames. Dora, who was cultivating a surfing style that was at once deft, contained, and nuanced with a graceful stealth, was referred to as "the Cat."

Although he developed a rapport with the other kids who started showing up at the beach (notably Ricky Grigg and Greg Noll, who was learning to shape balsa boards down in Manhattan Beach under the tutelage of Dale Velzy), Miki's stance was increasingly the joker and the outsider. Even so, the beach was their shared world, and the surf was the stage. Certainly the waves were Miki's stage. That's what he was living for – the waves and the art they elicited from him, and the freedom they allowed him to experience and demonstrate. For Miki, surfing was the only thing that explained it all – explained even the unexplainable. Riding a wave was the ultimate metaphor as well as the ultimate reality, the center of gravity of his very existence. It was an utterly transitory act, yet it was the thing that mattered most to him. Because it was absolutely in the present. It was Now, and Now required nothing but his undivided attention and a Zen spontaneity.

Everything important was at the beach – the waves, the sun, the girls, the sense of identity that was congealing around his surfing. The beach was his life. That's where he met Allan Carter during the mid 1950s; the two surfed together, discovered they shared a world-view and became best of friends. Like a lot of the surfers at Malibu, the two had access to levels of society not evident in the casual ambience of the shoreline. Indeed, the surf and sands of Malibu were on many a celebrity's A-list of getaways. Peter Lawford was a regular, and Zanuck's daughter Darilyn, and Tommy Zahn, who had courted Norma Jean. But apart from that, Carter and Dora had family connections that easily slipstreamed them into the most elite barrios of Southern California society. Thus did Allan summarize the Carter-Dora relationship: "We enjoyed riding waves and going to parties."

Still, a guy had to make a buck, and while he wasn't enamored of the idea of working for a living, Dora had some natural entrepreneurial skills … and the so-called gift of gab – his style was staccato, punctuated with odd turns of phrase, you see?

He started off as a parking attendant at the Beverly Hilton Hotel on the day it opened, August 12, 1955. He was a host at Villa Frascati Restaurant on Wilshire Boulevard not long after. He delivered wine for Alfred Hart Company, which got him started as a collector (he dug a small cellar behind Madam's house to stash his booty). Miki was even known to bring a female companion along on deliveries, which could then be interrupted for hilltop reposes and samplings of the wares.

Miki at Malibu, 1966. Photo Ron Stoner

Late in the spring of 1956, Tubesteak orchestrated a real career move for Dora. Tracey had been working as an underwriter for the Home Insurance Company, and when a trainee position opened up, he called Miki, who poured his tanned, reef-scarred body into a business suit and shoes and marched into downtown L.A. to make his fortune. But things didn't quite pan out. "Miki and I got shit-canned, " Tracey remembered, "him for drawing surfing cartoons of shmoos riding waves, me for having my desk drawers stuffed with Hollywood Park racing forms."

Tracey, suddenly without a paycheck and completely broke, figured he might as well just sleep on the beach, which he did. After awakening in the morning damp, he spent the next day harvesting palm fronds, driftwood, and assorted junk from the lagoon and built himself a shack to call home. It was the beginning of something.

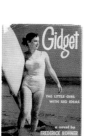

In June, 15-year-old Kathy Kohner (5 feet tall and 95 pounds) came to Malibu to learn how to surf. As her mother drove off, Kathy surveyed the scene: a pier, some waves, and a ratty beach shack with a half dozen or so young men hanging around with nothing better to do than accuse her of being a girl midget. And so it was that Gidget met Tubesteak, Scooter, Moondoggie, Golden Boy, and the rest of the gang. As her father would describe in the novel *Gidget*, the first-person recreation of his daughter's summer published in 1957, Malibu was one big party, orchestrated by Tracey, and it ran all summer long. And at the end of it, at Malibu's 1st Annual Luau, Tube torched his grass shack.

The following summer, it was the cops that tore down the shack. Apparently, the city fathers were concerned that the trend at Malibu wasn't entirely wholesome; after all, it was a public beach. Those summers of love – before the beats, before the hippies, and very likely anticipating both – were profoundly brief and retrospectively perfect, so the nostalgia for them became a powerful intoxicant to chroniclers of surfing history.

In fact, Dora's perfect seasons had already come and gone; he wasn't really a part of the Gidget thing; his surfing set him apart and defined the standard to which the others aspired. He was aloof, seemed

Ambassador for Frank Donahue's USOA, 1960. Courtesy Family of M.S. Dora

to think himself better than the others, and was beginning to show such a perverse pleasure in hassling his inferiors that he had begun to alienate himself. As for the authorities, they began to suspect that, though he was well-spoken and well-connected, he might well prove to be incorrigible.

> I drop in, set the thing up and behind me, all this stuff goes over my back; the screaming parents, teachers, police, priests, politicians— they're all going over the falls head first into the reef. And when it starts to close out, I pull out the back, pick up another wave and do the same goddamn thing. – MSD

At the very least, he was extremely opportunistic. Now calling himself Mickey Dora, he didn't do anything in the usual way. Allan Carter recalled that whenever Miki received tickets to some function, he would sell them then sneak in. An avid Monopoly player, Dora was frustrated that Carter was virtually unbeatable and would actually steal his deeds and funny money if Allan dared to leave the room. When he found himself in one of those take-a-number joints, Dora would find a stub on the floor, move to the front of the line, and ask why they hadn't called his number yet.

Carter sometimes referred to Miki as the Gypsy Darling. "Hungarian Gypsy blood," he explained. "Ramona looked like a Gypsy, and Miki was competitive and compulsive, but he was totally in control of his faculties. He just had a Gypsy mentality, unlike his dad."

Dora would prey on the clueless day-surfers who passed The Pit (a loosely defined area in the Malibu sand where the pack hung out) on their way down the beach. He hit them up for lunch money or to impound their surfboards or simply dish out a little verbal abuse in the spirit of Gard Chapin and Bob Simmons, both of whom had now, suddenly, vanished from this earth – Simmons drowning in big surf at Windansea off La Jolla in September of '54, Gard quite recently the rumored victim of murder or suicide down in Baja, Mexico. Who was left to carry the torch?

Frederick Kohner's 1957 novel, *Gidget*, it can be argued, was striking because it was written from a protofeminist perspective of someone who was a participant in the sport. Anyone who has ever read Kathy Kohner Zuckerman's original diaries will immediately spot the unmistakable logic and language that informed the novel, the subsequent series of motion pictures, and three television series. Malibu beach lore maintains that the girl-midget's (aka Gidget's) innermost thoughts, desires, and dreams were appropriated by her father and presented as his own work. Social observer Deanne Stillman has stated that the resultant book is extremely significant because it represents "the female *Catcher in the Rye*." Interpersonal dramatics and literary accolades aside, the empirical evidence supports the position that the Gidget phenomena is still the most debated aspect of the modern age of wave-riding. For some *Gidget* is great art, to others she is an Ameryiddish Cassandra who scrawled the demarcation line of the fall from grace. Whatever the case, things soon got worse.

Gidget, Ride the Wild Surf, Beach Party, Ski Party, Gidget Grows Up, television spots, and on and on... The iconoclast Dora served as a highly paid "surf stuntman" and thereby helped to midwife the bastardization of both his own solitude and ethical system. And he was also standing at the ready way back then, on that heated day in Malibu when it was his duty to serve. A preemptive strike was conducted in which bags of shit were dumped down the air-conditioning ducts of *Gidget* director Paul Wendkos' Cadillac Sedan de Ville. Theoretically, this exercise might be interpreted as falling into the domain of a technical adviser. Could the auteur have captured the fetid essence of Malibu Point's sphere of socialization without this crash course in aromatherapy? Did Dora do enough or do too little in his position as protector of the faithless?

For a time, he was considered a promising young actor and had serious industry interest in his prospects. Miki's dadaesque sense of the absurd allowed him to monkey-wrench the Tinsel Town proceedings by day and to enthusiastically plunder the town's A-list hot spots by night. The rising son frequented such venerated Angelino bistros as Dan Tana's, Chasen's, The Brown Derby, La Scalla, and the Spanish Kitchen. He rallied his troops and blitzkrieged countless society functions, cinema premieres, political events and bohemian soirees. Clubs like Chez Jay, Trader Vic's, the

Fifth Estate, Mocambo, the Coconut Grove, Ciro's, the Daisy, and the Whiskey A Go-Go noted his presence and oftentimes took extra precautions to ward off the volatility of the wrecking crew that traveled in Da Cat's wake.

But this was Los Angeles improper, where herds of industry trophy ingénues tanned their hides along the beaches of the Crescent Bay. Where girls achieved more by doing less, men would do anything to assure a career in the movies, and Miklos Sandor Dora was "discovered" so many times that he had to work overtime to get lost. — CRS

On April 10, 1959, Columbia Pictures released *Gidget*, starring Sandra Dee as "the little girl with big ideas" and Cliff Robertson as Kahuna, the surf "bum" who lives in a shack on the beach. The real Kahuna, Tubesteak, was hired as a technical consultant and had a minor (and uncredited) role in the film. Ironically, Dora's involvement in the flick was doubling in some surf scenes for James Darren, who costarred as Moondoggie; the irony being that Moondoggie was the nickname assigned to Billy Al Bengston, a genuinely great artist but perhaps the least skilled surfer in the vintage Malibu pantheon.

Adapted from Kohner's novel by a television writer (Gabrielle Upton), the movie spun a romantic tale of a free-spirited clan of rebel hedonists who lived, loved, and surfed on the beach, disdaining conventional society. Somehow, it hit the American youth audience right where it counted, and word spread quickly: *Gidget* was released in Finland on July 31st of the same year.

As if divinely orchestrated, in the midst of a shortage in the supply of South American balsa, between the publication of Kohner's novel in 1957 and the release of the film in 1959, polyurethane foam revolutionized surfboard production. Suddenly foam-core surfboards could be manufactured in less than half the time for less than half the raw-materials cost of wooden boards. Thus, with *Gidget* drawing thousands of new enthusiasts to surfing, the board-builders were ready for them, and the "surfboard industry" was born.

So it was that surf culture exploded into mainstream consciousness and, as it did, brought Miki Dora ever closer to a crisis of polarities. The takeover of Malibu by Tubesteak's rat pack had left him out in the cold, and the subsequent Hollywood spin on his own briefly private slice of Eden had him swooning, but worst of all he'd been party to it, doubling for Moondoggie. Dora had to examine his own pragmatism here, had to cut to the chase and see where this was all going.

But … what could it matter? He could see the writing on the wall. Already he was surfing more at Topanga, the next point south of Malibu. The waves weren't as perfect as Malibu's, but the riff-raff didn't have access. His own particular right-of-way was through a private gate in back of Jim "Fitz" Fitzpatrick's house. The Fitzpatricks lived on the second floor and rented out ground level to a young surfer named Bill Cleary. Fitz was a film director and editor who would publish *The Surfing Guide to Southern California*, authored by Cleary and Dr. David Stearn, in 1963. His son Jimmy was a hot young surfer to whom Dora was always respectful and encouraging, a kind but mischievous uncle.

"He really loved to surf," the younger Fitzpatrick recalled. "He was always hassling me if there were waves and I wasn't surfing: 'Hey man, what're you doing? Get out there and surf! Don't take it for granted, kid.' He'd make me go out surfing with him, and then he'd encourage me to take off in front of him." Jimmy ("Jim" after his father passed) became a life-long friend of Dora and never personally experienced the darker side.

"For about two years, from '60 to '62, we had Topanga virtually to ourselves," Jim recalled with some amazement. "Those were incredibly influential times – no magazines, no pictures, just live surfing … even at Malibu I can remember times surfing with Cleary and Miki – shoulder-high sets and just the three of us."

Everything exploded in 1962, and unless the surf was extraordinary, Miki rarely went to Malibu. That was also the year Matt Kivlin hung it up; as a stylist himself, he'd had considerable influence on Dora,

but the crowds that summer broke his spirit.

"Miki was angry and pushing in the water that year," said Fitzpatrick. "The idyllic experience was gone. And it wasn't gradual; it was night and day. It was an incredible feeling. It was over."

Samuel Z. Arkoff (*Beach Blanket Bingo*, *Muscle Beach Party*, etc.), as conductor of American International Films, concocted his own version of the tableau vivant. His insidious plot worked off the fears and insecurities of the baby-boomer consumer class. Arkoff's bastardized sand and sea project came out of the purest of motives – the impulse to create disposable drive-in films mired in teen angst specifically geared for a ripe market of suburban children. American International's perfected formula was to mix maudlin sentimentality, sun, surf, sex, cars, motorcycles, body fetishism, fad, fashion, fantasy, music, and anxiety into celluloid stew. – CRS

I knew every one of the chubby flaccid pretenders. I did everything I could to screw them over and sabotage their methods. It was me that taught Sally Field how to make-believe surf. I liked her. The Flying Nun just about drowned in a sea of back projection. Wrecks of child stars washed up on soundstages gasping for air. These farmers were so out of place, their agents never told anyone that they did not know how to swim. The Hall of Shame was crowded with talent dreadfully acting like they had ever seen the ocean: Denver Gilligan, Ricketts Rickles, Tabby Hunter, Catalina Frankie Avalon, and Anita Mousecatello. Directors would try to lay anything brown and lithe on the casting couch. There were many so-called wave riders who were in heat for this process. The challenge to the educated was to turn down the Tinsel Town lucre. A livelihood could be made of renting yourself out to these charlatans. I pressed the pass line and got by, or so I thought. Once I was sick as a dog from a rancorous case of dysentery I'd picked up in Mexico. On camera they're filming this sad-sack party scene with some Philly cheesecake crooner up in the spotlight, and I'm in the background puking. The director calls out, 'Hey, dark kid in the back, I like what you're doing. That's a marvelous look. Save it for the next scene.' I knew I was kaput then.

There were other ways forthright individuals dealt with them. It was easy to get on the call sheet and then bail for the day and have a confederate sign out for you at golden hour. Many got paid for overtime when they were never there anytime at all. The reliable low-lifes would rifle the purses and wallets in the stars' dressing-room trailers. Another preferred routine was to be issued a brand new board from the prop department and to then paddle out around the rock into the hidden cove, where there was a stash of terrible broken five-buck trash boards from Louie Shell's hock shop. Switcheroo shenanigans went on like this every day, and no one ever cared enough to catch on. The Terrible Twins got one of their string of teen comfort girls to allow herself to be seduced by a septuagenarian producer. A Bolex hidden in her boudoir recorded the dirty rendezvous. When they arrived at the mark's estate to collect their hard-earned extortion money, the LAPD apprehended them. The producer then sold a chronicle of the escapade as a screenplay. The soul-sucking Hollywood harlots were bigger thieves than any of us. They even ate their own kindred spirits. Buster Keaton was being held prisoner on the set of *The Horror of Enema Beach* or some such excremental whopper [*How to Stuff a Wild Bikini*]. I got to know him and discovered that he was a genius working so far beneath his true station that it was ghastly. Keaton had once been the number-one box office draw in the movies, but by the time we became acquainted he was forced into living on a chicken ranch out in Nowheresville. It was not even that high-quality – Canoga, Winnetka, Tarzana, Cucamonga … Buster's coop wasn't even on the train line. But he didn't care because he still maintained his dignity.

My father had a number of friends who were writers, directors, and playwrights – King Vidor, André De Toth, Paul Lukas, Vincent Korda, Andre Arto, Geza Herczeg and Michael Curtis, George Cukor. They were the intellectuals of the industry. Errol Flynn used to come over to our home and taught me to swordfight. Pancho Gonzales and Don Budge played tennis with my father. These men were the genuine article, and the movie businessmen worshipped their skills just as they resented them for having these same attributes. The women in the business my father knew had it worst of all.

Hedy Lamarr, Greta Garbo, Veronica Lake, and Marlene Dietrich – they were the objects of desire, and the moguls treated them shamefully.

My stepfather had grown up around the area and was well connected, too. The fact that he was a dangerous psychopath helped earn him respect wherever he went. So you could say I grew up knowing the nature of the beast.

Captain Frank Donahue [Hollywood director and a founder of United States Overseas Airways] worked me into a commercial, and he showed me the ropes on how to handle Hollywood. Frank was a specialty director that was another friend of my stepfather; he was a scurvy, freebooting pirate who had trained sharks for Howard Hughes. Frank would catch them in the ocean and haul them to Hollywood where he'd throw the poor things into a studio tank. Catch was, the pool was filled with fresh water, and the sharks died instantly. Old Hughes was convinced that Cap had screen-educated a solitary shark and that it was all being accomplished via animal acting. Different sharks would jerk and spasmodically twitch until they croaked. Captain Frank then would yell "Cut!" and go to work with the fish. The wankers were stiff and belly up. Donahue's boys would bring in another one, and the show went on. The millionaire loved this and never caught on to the switching and paid off big.

My gag was on some piece of crap TV thing, I don't remember. A unit director took me aside. "Hey Feeler, follow my lead. Surf behind the boat until I give us the signal then fall off the tail of your board and shoot it at the cameraman."

I was concerned. "Won't he get hurt?"

"Do you want this job? Then just do as I say. I'll cover you later."

It went down like he said, just as subtle as a mule kicking the sides out of a tin barn. The board corkscrews through the air, nails the boat, and the director pushes the camera operator out of the way. Now he is suddenly a big hero; he saves the guy's life. But the camera gets deep-sixed overboard, and production has to shut down. The producers leave very upset because the Panavision camera that went into Davy Jones' locker is worth hundreds of thousands of dollars.

The Pit. Malibu, 1961. 16mm Grant Rohloff

"Hey Coach, what are we gonna do now?"

"Do you want to earn a bonus, Junior?"

The unit director tells me to dive down and grab the camera. I wrangle it up; he pulls it into the boat and douches it with a bucket of clean water. The insurance policy pays off on the Panavision; he sells/returns the camera back to the studio. We work for another three days with a hazardous-duty stunt bonus. That job indoctrinated me into the gestalt of the law of the sea, salvage rights, and set etiquette. — MSD

Wit, wisdom, or circumstantial coincidence. What drove Dora through the counterculture? Venice was loosely at the epicenter of his ramblings. Gard Chapin was a connected cultural outsider by disposition who had many watermen from this beach in his sphere of activity. The primary connection? Mary Donahue, mother of his friend Michael Donovan, was a sportswoman from down by the canals. Her second husband, Frank Donahue, had lifeguarded in this general vicinity where George Freeth had first set up shop after coming over from Hawaii. Freeth's reknown as the introducer of surfriding to the continent was based on what happened there. Cal Porter was the Venice-born guard who pulled first duty at Malibu Point. Tulie Clark graduated from guarding and living on the old Venice pier to founding International Surfing Magazine and owning the first house on Malibu Point. And Michael's wife, Toni Donovan, was by profession a fine artist's model, who was a confidant and subject to imagists like John Altoon, Don Bachardy, and Christopher Isherwood.

Dora was a fixture at counterculture rites, going to the Gas House in Venice to hear poets backed by Chet Baker; to view Bobby Troup and Julie London at Shelley's Manne Hole; to Gordon Wagner's assemblage shop on top of the Effie Street steps; to bet the ponies at Santa Anita with Charles Bukowski; to see Lightning Hopkins at Xanadu; to the Sunset Strip riots at Pandoras Box; to the Barrel House in Watts to dig Johnny Otis; to Topanga to Edmund Teske's; to the Lighthouse in Hermosa to see Wes Montgomery; to readings at Jake Zeitlan's, Papa Bach's, Dawson's, Bridge, and

Dora taps intruder. Malibu, 1966. Photo Brad Barrett

Baroque, where he would debate literary metre, simultaneous alternative meaning, and contrapuntal rhythm with Billy Pillan, John Fante, Jack Harris, Ward Ritchie, Jack Smith, and Jim Murray; to the Beverly Cavern Club to listen to Tommy Tedesco; to the Avalon Ballroom in San Francisco with Rick Griffin as a guest of Bill Graham; to the Shrine Auditorium next to giant Felix Chevrolet, where someone unleashed several cages of Ex Lax-dosed cats that rapidly disrupted the sonic reveries of the Grateful Dead; to the Cheetah on Lick Pier, where the aspiring actor Judas Johnny would claim that Da Cat tried to kiss him on the dance floor, thus revealing the thespian's misunderstanding of the traditional kiss given to a betrayer; to greasy-spoon breakfasts including one at Olivia's Place in Ocean Park with Admiral Morrison's son, Jim; to serenades up on the deck near Red Rock performed by the Governor's disguised daughter and Bernie the Eagle; to paint in the Broad Beach atelier of Anthony B. Heinsbergen; to hang out in the parking lot of Vinyl Fetish with Exene Cervenka and John Doe; to attend a myriad of salon exhibitions featuring art works by such links as Ron Cobb, Kenneth "Greenwater" Price, Stanton MacDonald Wright, Richard Peterson, James Ganzer, John Altoon, Robert Irwin, Karen Carson, Joe Goode, Billy Al Bengston, Rick Herold, Ed Moses, Fidel Danielli, Robert Irwin, Helen Frankenthaler, and Wallace Berman; to Helm's Athletic Hall in Culver City with Bob Simmons to feel the balance of Jimmy Foxx's bat and to determine its grain pattern; to visit the historical fossil archive in the basement of the Los Angeles County Museum of Natural History, and so forth. – CRS

Just a few of years earlier, Kerouac's *On the Road* had been published (1957) and the so-called "beat" scene of poetry, jazz, and art had erupted in New York, San Francisco, and Venice Beach, California, where, near the ruins of Abbot Kinney's turn-of-the-century vision, Miki spent time at the Gas House and the Venice West Café diggin' on the hipness of his fellow man and finding his groove. But surfing was nothing; it didn't exist yet, outside of a couple of thousand participants and a few annual surf documentaries that toured legion halls and high-school auditoriums. Now all that was changing, and you had to either thank or curse Gidget for it. Or Dora.

Less a victim of the times than a catalyst, he was a fusion artist riding that wave, calling forth all those changes – exotic in speech and dress, edgy in thought, experimental with hallucinogens, lusting for fast cars … lusting for life.

> My only regret is that I did not torch Gidget's palm-frond love shack with that phony fafoonie and Tubesteak and Minnie the Mongoose and Jerk Off Johnnie and all of the rest of the cast and crew inside. What a glorious imu oven it would have made. We could have had a kamaaina luau with Hollywood long pig as the main course. The Hawaiians ate Captain Cook; it is unfortunate that the rest of us at Malibu learned so little from these gallant combatants. – MSD

In 1960, surfer and former art teacher John Severson published the "First Annual Surf Photo Book," titled *The Surfer*, as a program for his new film, *Surf Fever*. Demand was so great, he turned it into a quarterly periodical, then went bi-monthly as *Surfer* magazine. Other surf-niche periodicals followed, notably *Surfguide* ('63–'65), which was edited by Cleary. Severson's magazine was published in Dana Point, near San Onofre, and the two publications soon found themselves in competition for readers and advertisers. *Surfguide* was making strong gains on *Surfer* when Cleary ran a cover story on "Malibu Characters and Waves" in the November 1965 edition. The cover shot – Miki, Aaberg, Mary Sturdevant, and Lance standing in front of the famous Adamson estate wall at Malibu. Inside, Cleary's first published interview with Miki and other Malibu surfers broke ground in the new world of surf journalism, and the mag's mailbags filled with subscription checks.

Dora: The vintage years are over. I have my memories and that's it. I want to keep them to myself. I don't want to share them with a bunch of idiots …

Henry Ford: Seeing this place at its birth, like Mickey did – seeing five or six surfers out and all of them good: Matt Kivlin, Bob Simmons and the others, and seeing it change to what it is now (never less than 50 to 150 Valley Cowboys pushing and shoving, going straight off and calling him a *kuk*) – I can see how he's disgusted. I know I am.

Dora: In the Kivlin era they had a hard-core clique. After Simmons died and everyone got married, everyone settled down and the Tubesteak era came into being. They sat on the beach and made their surfboard talk. That's when I had my best time (from '55 to '58) and I had about three or four years there all to myself. As for the group, I wasn't in … I wasn't out. I was just accepted there. I was accepted for my wave-riding – not for my personality.

Dewey Weber: The first time I saw Dora? No matter how far back I think, I can't remember a time when all of a sudden there was Dora on the beach. It just seems like he was always there …

Kemp Aaberg: When I first saw Dora I was this little white *kuk* at Malibu,-and this guy went by and I didn't even know who he was. I just saw him go by. He was dark and agile, but I really didn't know whether he was good or not. All I knew was he could move and I couldn't. Mickey is one of the best. He lives a unique, non-conforming life, and people follow him like sheep. But there's no one around like him. He's the one. … I think the crowds sicken him more than other people. He's one of the few guys who really loves to surf.

Dora: Malibu is summer . . . summer is ruined. Now you have to share your summer vacation with every-body – I hate to share my time with working slobs. Summer has had it. You have to share it with everyone else. Now I hate summer: for four months out of the year now I have to sweat it out.

All this was completely unprecedented and belied the fact that Dora had continued to do stunt work

Dance party scene from a beach movie. c. 1960. Courtesy Family of M.S. Dora. Photographer unknown

(surf) and play bit parts in a series of surfploitation films (*Beach Blanket Bingo*, *Beach Party*, etc.) produced by some of Hollywood's most questionable "artists". He was taking the payoff with one hand and flipping 'em the finger with the other. Anytime there was a beach flick in production, there was a sudden glut of recently repainted stock surfboards for sale. Of course, all along Miki also appeared in the low-budget 16mm surf movies being made by Severson, Bruce Brown, Grant Rohloff, and a dozen others. Rohloff was a fellow surfer from Hollywood High, and he had privileged access to Dora; his period footage was the most intimate of the young Cat.

But print media is different. For one thing, you get to say something, and you can get creative. The implications were not lost on Miki. The fates had dealt him a forked temptation. Suddenly he had media to magnify his impact, to explain himself, to tell his version of the story, to enlarge his message (whatever that was) and his stage. And it was fundamental, because no one knew what a real surfer was; no one off the beach had ever spoken to one, really. Miki was uniquely groomed for the celebrity; like no other surfer, he was there to optimize the situation. He was in position, and being in position, as every surfer knows, is the most important part of surfing.

After the demise of *Surfguide* in 1965 (precipitated by a $1 million libel suit threatened by Severson's attorneys), both Cleary and Dora migrated pragmatically into the pages of *Surfer* magazine, where Miki established himself as surfing's most controversial literary figure.

Social circumstance determines your running mates. Dora was there when John Lennon's cigarette case was nicked that night at the Beatles house on Bluebird Lane. And when Duke Kahanamoku's surfing hood-ornament statuette was pried off his Lincoln Continental. Miki would on occasion converse with Henry Miller on the beach. He'd been to parties at Sharon Tate and Roman Polanski's. Manson was first encountered behind the Raft Bar up at Topanga. The last time Miki saw Charlie was across the corridor while the two passed in transit while en torcida. Writer Jane

54

Hollister Wheelwright and Miki would discuss her personal interaction with Carl Jung while attending fandangos on her exclusive Gaviota surf ranch. Baron de Philippe Rothschild entertained his girlfriends. MSD showed Mick Jagger and Keith Richards the high ground when Joan Eldon's beach row house flooded. Elvis studied at Kealoha Parker's, and that's where Miki met Bruce Lee. The four of them would verbally dissect protocols of motion. Parker (the "magician of motion") was a protégé of Professor Thunderbolt Chow in Honolulu. Connected on that end were Rabbit Kekai and the Hotel Street cartel. Steve McQueen was around there, too. – CRS

Unbelievable motorcar bargains were available. I would pick up '30s coach-built luxury cars for almost nothing. They were these amazing great old machines laying around rusting, and no one thought much about them because after the war everyone wanted something new. They were cheap. Sometimes maybe I was getting them for too little as the cops were interested how a kid was coming up with these bombs. The Hot Rods to Hell creeps all over the city hated the sight of me. They'd be out cruising in their slow-boat Pachuco sleds, and I would fly past them in my souped-up V-12 1939 La Salle. Survival instinct required that I concoct a plan to foil the hillbilly hair hoppers who were after me. It had been raining so I dangled a strap of woven metal that went down from my distributor junction and touched a puddle on the street where I had parked. I'm sitting in my convertible outside of Hollywood High talking to a couple of chicks at lunch. The lunkheads see me charming their goo-goo girls and they are out for blood. The entire school is watching because they know I'm going to get it. The head thugs run up to my car door and bingo, I've got them right where I want them. I hit the switch and an electrical jolt travels down the strap and across the puddle and right into these dolts. Zap bap a lop a dop a bop bam boom. These retards were so stupid that they couldn't comprehend what was happening to them. The car was grounded because of its rubber tires. Victory was mine. – MSD

McQueen recognized Dora from the nascent car scene in Hollywood when both were delinquent

youths. Back in the day Miki bought Rolls Royces from elderly screen sirens and sold them to socialites in San Francisco. The Hollywood Auto Theft Division of the LAPD kept tabs on the ever-expanding graveyard of Pierce Arrows, Talbot Lagos, and Packard Phaetons parked outside of grandmother DeSanctis' house.

For a challenge, Miki would drop Briggs Cunningham-prepped racing motors into unlikely plain-Jane vehicles. For money, he'd cruise up to Mulholland Drive or out to Sepulveda Canyon to engage in street racing. A keen driver, he moved in the quickest circles so he could assure he was outfitted with the best. He piloted Scarab road racers courtesy of his accomplice in overdrive, Lance Reventlow. Miki was a semi-irregular around Reventlow's Venice fabrication facility while the first Formula One car ever produced in the United States was being built up. Dora was also later observed haunting Carroll Shelby's Cobra works in the same setting. An employee at Santa Monica's Lincoln-Mercury dealer was reportedly the mysterious benefactor who granted Dora access to Mangussos and Panteras, which he contested in Banzai runs.

Over the decades, one way or another, Dora dug up the sponsor dollars necessary to campaign a series of provocatively sophisticated and exotic high-performance automobiles. His garage housed such swift examples of the milieu as 1948 Jaguar XK120, more than one Porsche 356 Speedster, 1953 Mercedes Benz 300 Mille Miglia Sport Leicht, 1956 Rometsch Beeskow, 1958 Porsche 350A Spyder, and a 1968 Lotus Coventry Cosworth-powered race car.

Perchance the best gage of Dora's obsessive pursuit of high-velocity neutral handling was his liking for hurtling the Lotus through the abandoned streets of the central city's skid row at 2 a.m. He alleged that, "the air provided perfect aspiration at that hour, and the winos were well-lubed and performed nimbly as human pylons." – CRS

A sideslip on a surfboard properly executed is very much like a great sports car thrown into a four wheel drift. Pushing it in and pulling it through with all of the unweighting and down-biting. Heel and toe techniques control both. – MSD

He was reputed to be a double-talking scammer, a petty (and not so petty) thief, and a sociopathic opportunist, but worst of all, Miki Dora was rumored to be nothing more than a small-wave surfer. Since the early 1950s, surfers had been raising the bar in Hawaii's winter waves, but Miki played little part in the evolution of big-wave surfing. He'd stowed away on a cruise ship to Hawaii back in 1953, made it as far as the Honolulu jail, but he'd only really been there once since. So when he was hired as stunt double for Fabian in the Hollywood production of *Ride the Wild Surf* (1964), he approached the situation with some trepidation; nonetheless, he rode the important North Shore spots – Waimea and Sunset Beach and even the Banzai Pipeline. After some adjustments, he surfed well and even confidently – so much so that he was one of only 24 surfers in the world invited to the inaugural Duke Kahanamoku Invitational the following winter at Sunset Beach.

Despite all of this, Dora was getting ever more cynical about surfing and spending more time away from the beach, which held little charm for him now that it was teeming with new-found enthusiasts, and when he did surf it was at more obscure and uncrowded spots, like Santa Monica State Beach and Topanga. Yet the more he pulled away, the more the surfing world wanted him. He was inducted into the International Surfing Hall of Fame, the filmmakers wanted him in their surfing movies, and at a time when a number of the top surfers were making money off "signature model" surfboards for the big manufacturers, he decided to bite the bullet on that one, too, introducing Da Cat, a limited-edition surfboard, with a level of hype, satire, verbal abuse previously unseen in surf-magazine advertising.

In fact, though manufactured and sold by Greg Noll (now known as Da Bull and the world's most famous big-wave surfer, with the biggest surfboard operation), the idea for the spoon-nosed Da Cat had come from Reynolds Yater, a Malibu surfer and boardmaker, who had migrated north to Santa Barbara to avoid the crowds. "I made the board in the summer, and there were no waves, so I loaned it to Miki to test at Malibu," Yater later recalled. "The spoon wasn't a great noserider, but it was a great trimmer – lower

Topanga Beach, 1961. Courtesy Family of M.S. Dora

center of gravity. You could work it back and forth sideways, just the way Dora liked to surf."

Miki liked the board and suggested Yater release it as a Dora model, but there was no way Renny was going to go into business with Miki. In the end, Miki took the board to Noll, whose forte was delivering practical jokes and especially delighted in toying with Miki's hypertense persona. Who else but someone of Greg's mass could begin to handle Da Cat? Only Da Bull.

Together, Cat and Bull copied it and modified the Yater board before Dora sold it off, unfazed that it was one of Renny's special projects. But Miki immediately complained that the modified board didn't work like the spoon had. "He tried to buy it back from the guy, but he wouldn't sell," chuckled Yater years later.

Two years later, in 1967, Greg and Miki came to an agreement on a second Da Cat series, and for decades after Noll enjoyed regaling listeners with the tale of Dora's attack of buyer's remorse: "He was counting the money three times over. He sat there with a pile of sworn statements, notarized documents, escrow papers, every demand met, signed, sealed, and certified, nothing to bitch about, and finally he had to sign just three documents, and he sat there with the pen in his hand, sweating, hyperventilating, looking around the room like a caged animal."

By this time Miki'd been interviewed by all the surf magazines and was universally referred to as "surfing's angry young man" or "the Black Knight." In a piece titled "Surfing Stuntman" for *Surfer*, the question was put: "You've been accused of being ruthless on waves. What do you say about that?"

"It's a lie. I'm vicious," corrected Miki. "Actually, these guys are thieves and they're stealing my waves. If I get it first, it belongs to me. It's like a football scrimmage and every-one's blocking and tackling and every once in a while, you go for the touchdown. We're all pushing and shoving, jockeying for position and if I get the wave first, if I'm in the best position, then I feel I deserve it. In Malibu we have certain problems. These beaches up north are fairly crowded. So, when someone catches a wave I'm involved in – when he takes off in front of me – well, he's stealing my wave. He puts me in a position of either losing my

"...designed to obliterate...all the tuberoonies that come his way."

Photo for 'Da Cat' ad, 1966. Photo Pat Darrin

board or going into the rocks. So if he's in my way – well, he gets tapped. And then I get the blame and people say I'm pushing my weight around."

Many a surfer could empathize with Dora, so there was genuine appreciation for his acid wit and offbeat wisdom, although most readers probably fit the category Miki was defaming.

In that same interview he was asked about Hawaii. "How about it? I'd rather go to Selma, Alabama. There's too many hard feelings over there."

But he went back to the Islands, performed respectably, and accepted his Oscar-style trophy from Duke Kahanamoku, the father of modern surfing. While he made a repeat appearance the following year (and parodied himself beautifully in a classic car-chase scene for MacGillivray Freeman's new film, *Free and Easy*), he remained self-admittedly leery of big waves. "The whole North Shore keeps my adrenalin boiling," he told *International Surfing*. "Sunset Beach, Waimea, and the Pipeline all shake the cockiness out of me."

Making use of print media as no surfer had done before, he opened that same interview with an unprecedented disclaimer: "Before we start ... I just want to say ... that you people approached me for this interview. This has been the rule throughout my career; it's against my principals to seek out publicity. I made my reputation on my own ability in the water, not by hot air magazines. For those who are left of my dwindling following, who understand me and what I have to say, I just want to point out I'm making these guys pay for every word."

Miki thought the most accomplished surfer of all was Jack "Murph the Surf" Murphy, who in 1964 copped the 563-carat Star of India sapphire from the New York City Museum of Natural History. *The New York Daily News* reported it as "a chapter in criminal history that rivals anything in fiction." Dora considered the most maligned surfer of accomplishment to be 1993 Nobel Peace Prize winner Kary Mullis. *Time* magazine said, "Mullis became a beach bum, a surfer and also took a lot of LSD." Miki knew about acid from the good doctors at the UCLA Neuropsychiatric Institute, who liked to dose surfers to test their hand-eye coordination and balance while in altered states. Dr. Timothy Leary had Miki on stage as a performer during his Freak Out at the Santa Monica Civic Auditorium. Doctor Tim would later claim to be "the evolutionary surfer." Jimmy O' brought tons of peyote buttons out from the Southwest, where he was a tribally-licensed trader. – CRS

Clearly, the circus was in town, Dora had major cachet, and Malibu – let alone surfing – was nothing like it had been a mere decade before. His sense of violation and outrage was so apparent, it was getting easier for him to find his creative voice. He was strongly affected by the death of John F. Kennedy in 1963, and he continued to be disillusioned by the enormous blindness of his fellow man. So it was curious to find a strange note of optimism in this discourse on Malibu, which appeared in a 1967 edition of *Surfer:*

There I was killing time in my semifinal heat as some idiot water skier churned up the wave. Time was running out and with it my utter frustration with the high tide junk. I was observing the crowd on the beach, as I do on many occasions – what a fantastically picturesque place with the beautiful hills in the background. I was remembering how things were before the subdividers, concessionaires, lifeguards – before exploiters polluted the beaches like they do everything else.
I found the crowd very interesting. There was something I had never seen before in surfing. Aside from the ugly tourists and TV, there were the usual surf dopes, magazine and photo exploiters, the lap dog surf star club rah-rah boys, the same old story year after year.
But toward the point, strange, strange things were happening, faces and people I knew casually over the years with new costumes and appurtenances, maybe new philosophies. Something in their euphoric chemistry has been transformed into a new dimension. I can't put my finger on it exactly, but I begin to comprehend and come around. This subject is difficult to discuss openly, for I'm not an authority on human nature. If anything, I'm a freak of nature and don't fit in with anybody.

Miki with Duke Kahanamoku. Photographer unknown

However, I can't help feeling there's something happening and things are not going to stay the same. New philosophies are taking hold. There is a great deal of change accruing in certain segments of the sport, and I hope you want the same things I want, freedom to live and ride nature's waves, without the oppressive hang-up of the mad insane complex that runs the world and this sick, sick war. Things are going to change drastically in the next year or so, for all of us whether we like it or not. Maybe a few will go forward and make it a better world.

These are incredible times. Thank God for a few free waves. — MSD

Dora held a unique and peculiar position, not only in surfing but in the strange new world that was unfolding out of the collective California imagination. Waves were the central thing, no mistake about that, but his palate had been educated in other areas as well. He took pleasure in female company, for instance, his appetites assuming, if not legendary status, at least a respectable level of involvement in the brisk social traffic of the time and place. In short, he was seldom found wanting for a good ride when the waves were down.

Since Miki banned research interviews with alcoholic surf stars or old girlfriends, the following are based on his own comments:

Dina lived with him for a time and swore Dora swore her to secrecy about the affair of which she told "only her closest friends"; everyone knew. Suzanne hosted in the Gold Dust Lounge south of the slot on Market; when Dora went to the Bohemian Grove summer encampment, Suzanne accompanied him; for his birthday she blessed him with the key to the access gate of the Olympic Club's oceanfront fairway. Rosa the Californio brought Miki to the fiestas, where they performed such elegant acts as La Varsouviana, La Jota, and La Contradanza; Dianne worked as a process server; she stayed for six months and schooled him in the proper preparation of legal documents. Kelly rushed to catch the plane for their Hawaiian rendezvous; Dora was aghast when he "discovered" her on the plane, while she was bewildered by his onboard assignation partner. Miki thought he was taking Melissa to a Mensa meeting but wound up at the Tuttle High prom in the

San Fernando Valley. Alicia's ancestors paddled plank canoes out to greet Cabrillo. While Dora was incarcerated in the 1980s, this person, recognized by the federal government as "a Most Likely Descendant" of the lost Tongva people that once occupied the Los Angeles basin and most of the off-shore islands, sent him water from Kuruvungna Springs. Kuruvungna translates from the native language into "the place where we are always in the sun." Dora had chosen to live in decidedly unchic West Los Angeles; he said he needed the distance from the ocean so that there was a continued sense of revelation when he made his daily pilgrimage there. The apartment on Gretna Green Way was close to that same fresh water source point, which the Anglos characteristically called by the different name of Wounded Deer Springs. Miki realized this was where the Indians had saved Portola's parched expedition by leading them to the water in 1769. The Spanish in their day had referred to the source as Las Lagrimas de Santa Monica, the tears of Saint Monica. The location suited Miki Dora well, and he maintained that the water of the springs helped him to recover from the adverse health impacts of internment. Alicia provided both sustenance and knowledge.

Doris' headquarters were in a corner of the old Crossfield China complex off of Olympic. Dora's surfboard laminator, Johnny Belmond, was half a block up the alley. Miki used to talk to Doris about her objective in life, which was to create realistic pliable breast prosthesthetics for other mastectomy patients. They spoke about her past, which included the design and manufacture of an anatomically improbable, tan, molded plastic statuette called Malibu Mille. Doris thought it was "funny to meet the real Mister Malibu."

Real Barbie slept in a van parked behind the Yater shop on State Street. Miki would listen to her rant about how her engineer father had appropriated her countenance and sold it to a toy company. Whether true or imagined, he felt her tale of appropriation was symptomatic of a much larger problem. Real Barbie subsisted on creamed corn gruel that they gave out over at the Salvation Army homeless shelter. Sixties sang-froid can be a bitch in a '76 Chevy Sport Van that's run out of gas.

Ava knew that 40 percent of all men spontaneously soil their pants when under fire. Miki liked her from the instant they found each other at Snofru's Red Pyramid at Dahshur. She enjoyed when they spoke together about their respective first times. Hers was in an arid region under the silver lunar radiance. A deal went bad so she went worse. Dora wanted to know if it stayed with her. Ava said, no, she'd "put it right away and went on." You can't count on much, but anyone who has got your back is a friend for life. Miki cherished the companionship and her high threshold of operational awareness.

Janet knew him from a revels at Peter's house on Palisades Beach Road. She was with him in the Embassy Ballroom of the Ambassador Hotel shortly after midnight on June 5th, 1968, when Robert F. Kennedy was assassinated. *The Santa Monica Evening Outlook* reported that Miki had been questioned by police regarding his presence there. Despite his complete exoneration, the relationship with Janet became strained.

Joan, a poet from London's East Mill Hill, thought Dora's manner of dress to be a trifle eccentric if not downright "pirandellian"; during their months together Miki togged up in Kihachiro Onitsuka sprint shoes with vintage shirts by Pierre Balmain and tweed suits by Theodora Van Runkle all topped by a Schutzstaffel leather duster. Myra was an Omicron fine nine that he squired to the bar at El Cholo on Western where the couple would encounter footballer Tom Harmon, "Old 98," the Wolverine All American; she later married a lawyer who became a county official, and Dora "got leisure for life" as he described it. Audri had a California politician for a father, and she had won several world surfing titles decisively; she rode Andalusian stallions with Dora through the Pyrenees mountains.

Nyarai was an accomplice from West Street in Durban. She'd come down with several other Bashona from Zimbabwe. Later, people would claim that Nyarai was the beginning of the end of him. When Miki looked back, he said that he'd go through all of it with her again.

Francoise, the linguist, lived in the 10th arrondissement near Le Nord train station; across town

De-trunked on the North Shore, 1961. 16mm Grant Rohloff

Buffalo Keaulana, Greg Noll and Miki. Don Ho on stage. 1965. Photographer unknown.

Fred Hemmings Jr., Miki and Greg Noll. 1965. Wakiki. Courtesy Family of M.S. Dora

dwelled Valerie, the customs broker. Neither knew about the other. When Miki was not around, each assumed he was in Biarritz with his chemin de fer partner, Rozamond, the Dutch dowager. Rozamond thought her principle competition for his affection was a painter in Vaucluse named Bernadette. All of these women were aware that Dora's involvement with the Rio de Janeiro design-er Juliana was ending badly and gave Miki the space to end the affair gracefully. – CRS

He was still calling himself Mickey Dora in 1968, when he brought a new manuscript to *Surfer's* editorial offices in Dana Point. He was accompanied by an 18-year-old kid named Craig Stecyk, a mix of protégé and wunderkind, who carried a large Kodak box of black-and-white photo prints, many depicting Dora surfing obscure breaks along the largely neglected urban shores of Santa Monica. Miki's opus, titled "The Crackerjack Conspiracy," marked a distinct evolution in tone while continuing his formidable assault on the unchecked entropy of the status quo. In his opening lines – which in cadence and vision occupied the psychic space of Ginsberg's famous poem, "Howl" ("I saw the best minds of my generation destroyed by madness, starving hysterical naked …") – Dora spoke from a new perspective:

"During a multitude of years on the California Coast, I've watched the once dominant individuals of our art phased out by an uncomprehending bureaucracy. In an apparently useless endeavor, I devoted my energies and thoughts to warn the unenlightened of the plight of the times. Now, the 'hardened' lifeguards with their extension of power fantasies, the oldies but uglies, and the thousands of other plebian fruit flies that compose the alleged surfing sub-sub-culture are forcing me to seek greener pasture. Bad omens are in the air."

Later in the piece, his wittier persona began to engage the subject matter (the collapse of everything good about California): "Let bygones be bygones; the bandwagon has passed and those with a common interest must unite out of necessity. Having found an island near Madagascar which offers pre-atlas thrust conditions (viz., a more consistent break than California sans the minus-mentality morons); I'm going into exile there. Since I am leaving, I have chosen to divulge the last area on the Coast in which a person may exercise his wave-riding urge unhampered. I hope this knowledge will act as payment for any misunderstandings we have had between us over the years."

The payoff? Tips on surfing his secret Santa Monica backwater surf refuges. "As now must be evident to even the magazine-oriented, crawling, thinking substances, Santa Monica offers a splendid variety to those with the cranial capacity to truly take advantage of its abundant physical pleasures. Besides its natural resources, the area offers a well-seasoned blend of individuals. Spawned in the region's unique genetic pool resulting from years of isolation from the Mod Squad septic tank of the surfing world, they are devoid of the idiosyncrasies and juvenile personality cravings which usually are the rule. In exposing this spot to public scrutiny, it is my hope that aliens who venture into the realm will emulate this rare strain and, thus, upgrade the habits of wave riders everywhere. God save the king, for no one else will."

Dora had become a poet of lost hope, his eloquent paranoiac railing against the forces of mechanization and homogenization echoing literary rebels throughout history. Like many of them, he contained stunning contradictions: a mumbler of sublime eloquence, a macho artist (he was an accomplished pen-and-pencil man), a crude beach bum, a debonair denizen of high society, a small-wave rider who proved himself at Waimea when there was honor and money at stake. He was a rebel without a cause, but with causes.

"What he said made sense," admitted Yater. "He was always trying to draw attention to what he said with his odd way of vocalizing, and he was hard to understand, but his opinions were quite right, quite accurate – about the Valley. And his response was to work 'em over in the water and work 'em over in the text."

Furtive, distracted, brilliant, and saying what no one else could or would, Dora's next piece was supposed to be an interview for *Surfer*, but part way through the process he said, "Just write down your questions and I will consider and answer them." A couple of weeks later the editors received a manila envelope containing a slim manuscript and a hand-drawn graph of a timeline chronicling the major epochs

of surf history (DEAD ORIGIN, GENSIS PERIOD, and ILLUSIONARY PROSPERITY), with the assassination date of Kennedy prominently noted, culminating in a vertical descent labeled CATACLYSM. Among the questions Miki had created and answered:

Why did you drop the name Chapin?

That is actually a personal family question, but I can tell you this much, Gard Chapin, a unique surfing frontiersman, either remembered or not, had a profound influence in my life. His untimely premeditated murder in Mexico can only be linked with his individualistic personality. For my own peace of mind I felt it would be safer to use my given name. However, I sometimes have misgivings on this decision.

Could you clarify these various periods?

The dead origins consisted of the 250-plus redwoods and their wined-out "T" square-build grapplers, who fantasized themselves to be the magnates of an illusionary Polynesian culture. Bicep flexes, ukulele playing, tight trunks and body grease typified the period. I've only mentioned this era since it is frequently portrayed and glamorized as the birth of the sport, etc. Those guys weren't concerned with the effective riding of waves, and people today should realize this. The genesis days were a time of innovation, creation, birth and individuality. The Recession embodies the passage of time from the Genesis period's end to the present. Essentially, mediocrity and rehashed mediocrity. To the unenlightened eye, things have constantly been progressing; however, close scrutiny reveals the modern world to be a mere illusion of opulence, grandeurs and good feelings. People currently are riding the calm before the storm, and have been lulled into such a false sense of security that they view current occurrences as if they possess some sort of solidified foundation. They are viewing illusions as truth. The Death is the fall of the above mentioned illusionary society, values and prosperity. It will also entail a general shattering of the weak.

Why do you feel this fall is going to occur in the near future?

The advent of "professionalism" to the sport will be the final blow. Professionalism will be

completely destructive of any control an individual has over the sport at present. These few Wall Street flesh merchants desire to unify surfing only to extract the wealth. Under this "professional" regime, the wave rider will be forced into being totally subservient to the few in control in order to survive. The organizers will call the shots, collect the profits, while the wave rider does all the labor and receives little. Also, since surfing's alliance with the decadent big business interests is designed only as a temporary damper to complete fiscal collapse, the completion of such a partnership will serve only to accelerate the art's demise. A surfer should think carefully before selling his being to these "people," since he's signing his own death warrant as a personal entity.

What will you be doing when you're 64?

If I'm to be so blessed. Probably, the odds are slight that I shall ever reach 64. If, however, any of you are so fortunate to survive the cataclysmic cave-in, I shall be more than glad to discuss it with you at that time.

Disenchantment with the increasing bureaucratic regulation of the oceanfront and his abhorrence of the blunt-force eco traumas inflicted upon his beloved environs by legions of interlopers motivated Dora to travel far and wide. He fled America and from 1968 onwards he increasingly embraced the expatriate experience, circling the globe repeatedly. Extended residence was taken up in France, Indonesia, Australia, South Africa, Indo China, New Zealand, and Madagascar. Side sojourns of increasing oddity were reported, and as usual Miki's explanations hinted at both indiscretion and insincerity. Or did they?

East Berlin: "I was interested in vergangenheitsbewaltigung and the buildings of Albert Speer." Prague for the Russian invasion of Czechoslovakia in '68: "I went for tango lessons in Wenceslas Square." Visiting General Augusto Pinochet Ugarte's Chile: "I went for the right pointbreaks; they turned out to be lefts." East Timor: "I thought I was in New Guinea hunting for cannibals, but the gun runners were hunting for me." Namibia's Skeleton Coast: "I was looking for seahorse bones; finding the diamonds was a complete surprise." Ceylon: "When I saw the LARS rocket come past

Sunset Beach. 1963. Courtesy Estate Don James

During the Genesis period at Malibu in the early fifties I had it all to myself. Years of perfection that were idyllic in their simplicity. It was so mesmerizing that I failed to see the dark days coming. The Hollywood hustlers from Philly with their Shakespeare-on-the-surf morality plays, the nurses from New Jersey going tandem with Encino proctologists, and the Milwaukee morons with the homosexual panic beer ads. One day I was driving down Sunset Boulevard and there's this large billboard with a wave photo, and I'm in it but covered up by a mug of beer. This plundered moment even had a hideous little ditty: 'Taste the freshness – you're on top, thundering water under blue skies. A mountain on the move. And you fly.' The bastards will try to take everything from you. It was no longer safe to escape out in the ocean. They were stealing that too. – MSD

Dr. Don James on Billboard featuring his must famous photograph. 1963. Courtesy Estate Don James

the plane, I thought it was Sri Lankan Independence Day." Cuba: "I was flushing out feral Deusenbergs from the old sugar plantations."

Dora's impregnable language and implausibly sincere explanations have prompted several acquaintances of his to hypothesize that this self-styled monk's wanderings were entirely too coincidental. Were there deeper covert behaviors in play? Or did he say it as it lay? – CRS

Miki Dora's travels, the never-ending tour of the Malibu exile, began soon after Robert Kennedy's assassination at L.A.'s Ambassador Hotel in 1968. Dora flew to France, toured the countryside, surfed, checked out the scene, and found it to his liking. Miklos, Sr. (now an associate with Baron Philippe de Rothschild) met him there, and they traveled to Bordeaux to pay respects and tour the chateaux. They journeyed to Budapest, where Miki met his grandfather for the first time, enjoyed the view from the once impregnable Eger fortress, then was waylaid by the Soviet Gestapo when Miki carelessly photographed Hungarian soldiers returning from Czechoslovakia after the suppression of the "Prague Spring" democracy movement. Dora's interrogation was unnerving, and he and Miklos were lucky to be allowed to leave the country. As their departing aircraft reached cruising altitude, Miki exhaled. "Finally," he told his father, "I can breathe."

Back in California, Miki knew that it was over. The question was how to get out – how to travel the world, explore its wealth of perfect waves, thousands of them at any moment, breaking on remote beaches, inviting his unique appreciation of their transient divinity? His first big adventure in this new realm was a real icebreaker.

Don Wilson was one of the better Malibu surfers and an enthusiastic scammer. He played blond pink-skinned Nordic to Da Cat's Slavic swarthiness, and it was likely the two could learn some tricks from one another. In 1970, Wilson came up with the idea of heading down to Rio de Janeiro for Mardi Gras,

enlisting Dora, Carter, and another Malibu surfer, Greg "Mongoose" Meisenholder, a good friend of Don, who crashed several Hollywood parties with Dora over the years.

"Don Wilson was the Pirate Captain," remembered Allan Carter. "He pulled us all down there." But it was Carter's connections that won them the entrée to the penthouse of the governor of Rio and admission to the Governor's Ball, then smoothed over the $50,000 worth of jewels that Dora paid for with a bad check. Allan's host covered the debt and never said a word about it, but Carter felt burned. "Miki," he said, "was like a chimpanzee on a motorcycle with a loaded shotgun."

The adventure continued on to Paraguay, Uruguay, Argentina, and the isle of Grenada and featured a series of run-ins, scams, close-calls, and fortuitous turns of events. Upon his return to Los Angeles, Dora wanted to sell the South America story to *Surfer* but was in no frame of mind to work on it. Carter was writing for the movies by this time and knocked out the story as a favor. "It was originally titled 'South America on $50,000 a Day,'" he recalled, "but Dora went back in and doctored it all up with his weird surreal shit. The photo of Martin Borman was actually some guy with his son on the Baltic."

"To Whom It May Underestimate" appeared in the October 1971 issue of *Surfer* and spun a surreal tale of their adventures in Rio, a visit to Uncle Kornell at the Gran Hotel Dora in Peron's Buenos Aires, and an uncomfortable excursion to the gothic estancia of one Señor B., a former Nazi who shows off his highly lucrative coca operation. Dora brings the story home with a final word to his readers:

"You must understand, my thoughts are with all you gentle people. The bankruptcy of your great country seems to be right on schedule. I guarantee the hypocrisy of the ecology lunatics will do an admirable job of cleaning up the rubble after the racial slaughterhouse free for all. But, please, I implore you, if anyone happens to find his way to Argentina, do not hesitate to call on me at any time. I would be jubilant to hear of the fascinating adventure of how you ever possibly escaped. Naturally, I will insist on your being my personal guest. Since the U.S. dollar is finished and not respected in this country and throughout the free world, do not be concerned, just bring a little old-fashioned wampum."

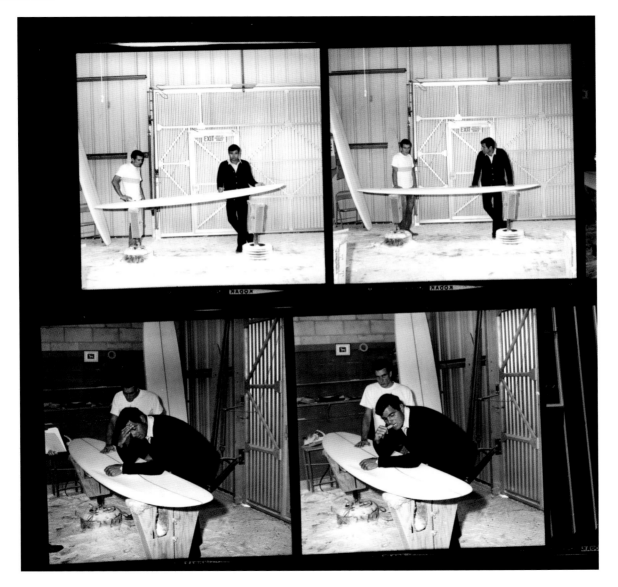

Once there were two men. Of the men that once were, I was once one. – MSD

That was the last word from Miki for quite a while. He gave himself up to the road, running the world with a moveable cast of characters and good friends. The means for his ends proved to be whatever it took; it was a wires-and-mirrors world of modified credit cards, forged traveler's checks, phony documents, passports, sweet talk, and misdirection.

Linda Cuy, who passed muster as a surfer and was nothing like Annette Funicello or Kathy Kohner, was Miki's lover for the next ten years, sharing his waves and his scams, getting close but never too close. She was a kitten with an agenda, and Dora loved his crime partner-sister confessor as only an individual who believed in nothing and adored no one could. She had his attention, and they ran together. On the sly, the pair pulled down the walls of jailhouses with a Land Rover, sequestered jewels in the hideaway heels of their boots of Spanish leather, and kited monetary exchange instruments into the stratosphere.

Her take on Ramona: "She was so beautiful it made her crazy." On Miki: "Surfing was absolutely the most important thing; nothing else mattered as much to him. Underneath it all, this man was tortured – tormented at military school, tormented at Catholic boarding school, tormented at Malibu, where he loved it but hated it, too. He wanted peace and quiet, but he also wanted the spotlight. The general public will never know him, really. They will never know the whole story."

Linda was Miki's match, and his accomplice. She went with him to New Zealand, and they kept going. "We traveled and got into trouble," she said. "Let's just say that I was doing a lot of artwork." But she never got caught. "I was always the one waiting outside the office at Interpol ... let me put it that way." For several years, she maintained simultaneous relationships with Dora and Don Wilson, whom Miki grew to despise.

While Linda was dividing her time between Miki and Don, Miki divided his time between Linda and

Marcia McMartin, the wealthy grand-daughter of a Scottish blacksmith who struck gold in the Rockies while working on construction of the trans-Canadian railroad. Thus the family fortune.

Marcia was about the same age as Miki, and he taught her to love travel. "He was quite influential in that way," she said. "He took me to exotic places, and he encouraged me to develop that side of myself." They went to South Africa, Thailand, Singapore, Bali ("all his trips related to surfing"), Australia, New Zealand, and a dozen other countries around the world. "I didn't surf myself," she admitted. "I was content to lie on the beach." When he was with Marcia, they didn't stay in vans. "We stayed in hotel rooms," she said, "and we split the cost of the room."

"People always gravitated to Miki," Marcia observed. "They wanted to tag along, be part of the legend. But I never saw Miki get into a fight or even an argument. He was a gentleman. It was Allan Carter who introduced us, by the way." Their relationship ended in 1975, but Marcia continued to have strong feelings, admitting that, "Miki was the love of my life."

Eventually, Linda burned out on living with Miki in a van in the southeast of France. "I couldn't adapt to the beachbreak waves at Hossegor and Le Barre," she explained, "so I finally told Miki I was going to Ireland to ride some good righthand point surf." Miki, for whom travel was restricted at the time (due to violations of court-ordered parole stemming from a bad-check-writing incident in Mono, California in 1973), was left in tears as she walked out the door with her surfboard.

One of Miki's best friends was Rick Peterson, a man with whom he'd found common ground. They'd met at the beach, of course, years before, and later, as they sat on their surfboards ("surfing, waiting to get poisoned or mugged, watching the turds float by and contemplating the antibiotics we would need to take immediately following our session," as Rick expressed it), escape seemed in order. Peterson was a painter in the Old Masters style, a devotee of elegance and an admirer of classical culture; his particular affinities included 17th-century Dutch art and painting techniques as well as Tudor- and Stuart-era English

culture and artifacts. He and Miki were very much in synch on their world views, shared a love of art, wine, fine food, skiing, surfing, and travel.

He recalled the two of them donning their tuxedos to crash the Biarritz Film Festival in 1979. Walking in "looking the part" and enjoying a fabulous meal, then adjourning to the auditorium for the awards. Anthony Quinn was going to speak, but then a man with a ski mask over his face and a machine gun in his hands took the podium. Rick and Dora noted similarly equipped associates at all the exits. "Miki and I just looked at each other, y'know – what do we do now?! They were Basque separatists. The man at the podium expressed his concerns, they left, and they showed the movie." Days later the two friends were skiing the Val d'Isere in the French Alps with complimentary passes. "I did some of my greatest work on those lift tickets," Rick remembered.

In 1981, Miki stepped into a phone booth in Guethary to make a call using a series of numbers that facilitated toll-free service anywhere in the world. Unfortunately, the same telephone was popular with those very Basque separatists and the booth was under surveillance. Dora was arrested and thrown into the Bayonne prison. Miklos was informed only after Baron Philippe noted the item in the newspaper and called his old friend. Miki was sprung, but asked to leave France; and when he arrived back in California, FBI agents were waiting.

Miki's past – or at least some of it – had caught up with him. He'd been arrested in Mono County back in 1973 for buying skis and equipment with a bad check, allegedly inadvertently, to help out a friend who had forgotten his wallet. He was charged with felony fraud but failed to appear and post bail as ordered. Subsequently, he changed his plea four times, finally pleading guilty on September 27, 1974. He got three years of probation and a $1,500 fine. He was prohibited from possessing credit cards, required to have a job, and an "approved" residence, plus he had to check in regularly with his parole officer.

Miki flew the coop. On April 11, 1975, the court issued a warrant for Miki's arrest for probation violation; bail was set at $10,000. After Miki was arrested by the French authorities in 1981, the outstanding warrant came up. He spent three months in prison in Bayonne before he could be extricated and evacuated. He flew home first class in September and was met at LAX by the FBI and taken directly to the Los Angeles County jail. From there he was moved to Terminal Island and then out to Bridgeport in Mono County, where he faced his probation-violation charges.

He pleaded guilty on October 6, 1981 and was given until January 2, 1982 to surrender, which he did. He was sent to a federal medical facility at Vacaville for diagnostic study, then returned to Bridgeport court to face the same judge that had tried him in 1973. Once again, he got three years probation along with the other conditions, plus was required to remain in California unless he got written permission from the court to travel, then was ordered to serve an additional 161 days in the Bridgeport county jail.

While serving his time there, the feds came knocking, took him to Denver to be tried on credit card fraud charges (forging a Diners Club credit card in 1969 and enjoying a two-year spending spree); facing a ten-year sentence, he plea-bargained and got six months back out West in beautiful Lompoc federal penitentiary, from which he was released on December 17, 1982.

Soon after Miki got out of custody, he visited Tubesteak's house in Lakewood, California for a barbecue. Tracey's teenage kids and their friends were so enthralled with Dora, they wanted him to take a bite out of one of their hamburgers. Tube's daughter wanted a picture of her dad with Da Cat, and Miki reluctantly agreed. When the photos were processed and Tubesteak was thumbing through them, he was shocked. "This is true," he recounted. "I saw the prints when they came back. The photos didn't show Dora, just me! He disappeared from the film!"

Like any rolling stone, Dora eventually found resting places on his journey, places to lay down his restless body and still his rattled brain – places where the quid and the quo were in some sort of balance. Biarritz and Jeffreys Bay became the residential poles of his residences in his last 20 years. He visited J-Bay, which is located on the southeastern coast of South Africa, for the first time in 1983 and was much impressed.

The following year, after golfing in Ireland, he acquired companionship in the form of a King Charles Cavalier Spaniel ("an eager, affectionate tail-wagger … lively, outgoing and sportive," as the experts say), which he named Scooter Boy after the legendary Waikiki beachboy. Miki always loved his dogs in a way that revealed a well of affection and playfulness he was reluctant to share with fellow humans, and Scooter Boy was his pride and joy. They became immediately inseparable, and he referred to him as his "son" and even enjoyed writing letters in Scooter Boy's voice. He said that when his son died, it would be the end for him as well.

Shortly thereafter, while visiting California, Miki was introduced to glass artist Ceci Clouse by a mutual friend in Laguna Beach. She was 29, Dora had passed 50, but the chemistry was good. She drove him to Trestles or Salt Creek or even San Onofre to surf, and out to visit Rick Peterson, who was living and painting in the high desert east of Los Angeles. "Rick was like a little Miki," Ceci said. "You'd see the identical mannerisms and expressions, the same way of talking. It was almost comical. They both loved great food and great wine … and great art. The two of them looked like they'd stepped out of a time warp, perhaps the King James period."

Ceci occasionally drove Miki to Santa Barbara to visit another longtime friend, Steve Taussig, whose Hungarian father had been a patron and friend of Miklos when he had the restaurant in Los Angeles. As she became familiar with Dora's personal history, she referred to his stepfather and father as "the rebel and the commander." She felt that the military and Catholic schools had "tweaked him" and that he felt abandoned by both of his parents." Coincidentally, Ramona lived nearby Ceci later in her life, but "he

97

didn't like to visit her when she had been drinking."

Ceci was fascinated by Miki's multiple personalities and amused by his phobias. Later, he would visit her at her estancia on the outskirts of Madrid. She asked for nothing, so he gave her everything in return. "People loved or hated Miki," she observed. "Most of the ones who hated him had encountered him in the '60s – they had a frozen image of him." She also felt that Miki was spiritual: "Surfing was his religion. He was very spiritual … especially toward the end of his life. Miki was one of the most complicated people I've ever know. He had to be super brilliant to deal with all of his contradictions."

Who shall win and who shall lose is ultimately determined by who keeps score. No good deed goes unpunished. No honest man makes it out alive. No one is allowed to pass unrepentant, at least on the official record. – MSD

Dora moved to South Africa in 1986, and although he still traveled rather frequently, during his extended hibernations in and around J-Bay, he was able to indulge an old and well-worn groove in his consciousness, because, like Malibu, the wave there is a long righthander, a classic point break with perfect wrapping faces, offshore breezes, a few surfers, a few leaping dolphins, a few lurking sharks … invigorating!

He rented a flat about 300 meters from a spot called Supertubes and generally kept pretty much to himself. An exception was playing tennis and golf with businesswoman Cheron Kraak, founder of the Billabong SA clothing company.

The attitude of surfer and writer Derek Hynd, whose house perched strategically over the beach at J-Bay, is instructive as to the unique position that Miki Dora occupied among those who more or less understood him. Hynd said that he'd come to count on Miki's frequent unannounced drop-ins with his "son" Scooter Boy: "They'd cruise through every couple of days, often when I was in the water, sometimes using the phone. It was nothing to worry about or let on. Regal bills just appeared like magic. To pay was

1964. Photo Peter Gowland

good. It was his right to extract tribute from me, you, anyone, anytime, anywhere. No sweat."

Periodically, he'd return to France or California. Following the so-called Longboard Renaissance of the late '80s, interest in Da Cat model soared and the boards were in great demand among collectors and retro-surfers alike. So, in 1996, Noll approached Dora about doing a third edition. In discussions triangulated by Noll's wife, Laura, who ranked as one of Dora's favorite people (witness the elaborate, carefully-crafted, and witty faxes he sent to her over the years), the two legends came together once again to create the most expensive limited-edition surfboard in history. Naturally, it was an immediate and enormous success.

That same year brought Dora a harsh setback. He had brought suit against Frontline Video to halt sales and have his likeness removed from a surfing documentary titled *"The Legends of Malibu."* He'd sought damages for the unauthorized use of his name, voice, and likeness. But the court determined that Dora was a public figure performing a public act in a public place and therefore not entitled to compensation. After all those years of perfecting his dance, developing his persona, finding his creative voice, his identity wasn't really his own after all. It was a shattering experience.

Then, in June of 1998, Dora's Jefferys Bay flat caught fire and Scooter Boy was killed. J-Bay surfer and board builder Andrew Carter told an East Cape News reporter that the fire started after Dora left a heater on under his bed. Carter said: "He was a total drifter. I spoke to him often. He was different to various people. I got on well with him. He was an interesting person – definitely an introvert." He said Dora did not take to people who treated him like a surf hero.

Real secrets will get you dead. I always forget to remember anything. I am a waterlogged sun baked old surf bum and that act always ends the inquisition. I wanted to be left alone. So I left alone. Now I don't want anything. – MSD

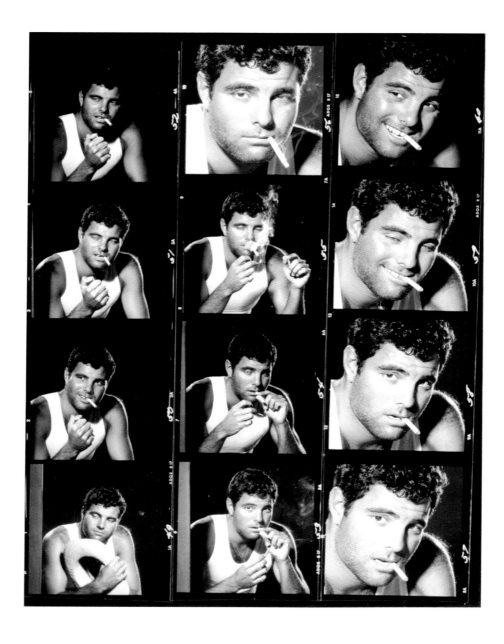

Dora had been pretty much gone from the scene since his departure from Southern California and the publication of his South American pseudo-saga. His only significant public exposure after that was in the movie, *Surfers*, in which he bravely rapped for Bill Delaney's cameras about truths and observations he knew the audience would be too clueless to grasp.

In 1989, a last, strange story from Miki appeared in *Surfer* magazine. Titled "*Million Days To Darkness*," the narrative seemed at once autobiographical and metaphorical. It was full of brilliance and ominous meaning, at once literal and surreal. In it, Miki journeys the west coast of South Africa, crossing through dangerous diamond-mining country and over the Namib border, following his own senses of adventure and destiny on a journey of discovery – of a great "episodic wave."

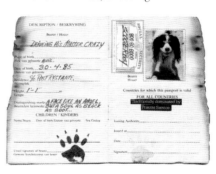

Finally, with Dora very much in the throes of a mighty struggle, caught in the grips of a powerful natural force, the tale ends abruptly … as if, like Coleridge, he'd awakened from an opium dream with misty visions of Kubla Khan melting into the ether. Or, even more so, like the abrupt nonconclusion of René Daumal's metaphorical novel, *Mount Analogue*. The piece was beautiful, witty, and important, but its author seemed to vanish at the end.

Waves are the ultimate illusion. They come out of nowhere, instantaneously materialize and just as quickly they break and vanish. Chasing after such fleeting mirages is a complete waste of time. That is what I choose to do with my life. - MSD

After the Jeffreys Bay fire and the death of Scooter Boy, Dora packed up what few possessions hadn't been destroyed and returned to France, feeling defeated and finished. He lived in Guethary in an upstairs room a couple of blocks from a small park with a couple of benches and an expansive view of the long tongue of reef that protruded out into the Bay of Biscay. He'd go down there to watch the reef trip the bands of swell that radiated in from the Atlantic and, if it was good, he'd go surfing.

Local surfers knew they could find him there, watching the waves, enjoying the light. They'd come by, greet him, pay their respects. He'd be polite, sometimes cordial. Some of them were friends he'd known for years. Everyone knew to give him space. There was a deference, a hush around him ... an aura of enigma. He'd be there, then he'd be gone – skiing, traveling, whatever – then he'd be back, sitting on the bench, looking out.

Miki Dora was an artist. He surfed as an artist would surf. Perhaps he was the first surfing artist, or the first *real* surfing artist. All his life he'd been a dancer in the Now, a man forever squinting into the glare of the moment. All his life he'd been busy creating moments, creating memory in himself and others. He had made things happen – situations, interactions, trouble – the way the beat poets did, the way that all holy fools do, because the thing was to Be Here Now. That's the essence of the dharma bum, and Dora was definitely a dharma bum.

Miki Dora was a philosopher, too. Dealing with complex internal forces pushes a man to occupy a higher place, disallows the possibility of believing one side of himself too much. What separates the insane from the saint, the delusional from the visionary? From the point of view of so-called normal, fixed-focus individuals, it hardly matters ... because "normal" people can't tell the difference.

"He was the sanest person I knew. Total sanity," said Nat Young, one of surfing's steadiest icons, and a solid friend of Dora's since they were booked into a room together at the '65 Duke. "He knew that the whole thing is a complete bullshit game that you play, and that you have to see the game for what it is."

Miki Dora wasn't perfect, but he had tendencies. There were long flat spells, where surfing was

Miki and Linda, Photo courtesy Linda Cuy

Miki and Baron de Philippe Rothschild. 1977. Courtesy Family of M.S. Dora

On "Grand Tour". 1972. Courtesy of Linda Cuy and the Family of M.S. Dora

Lotus series 7. c. 1970. Courtesy Family of M.S. Dora

critical to keep the juices flowing, to stay one step ahead of all the shit. But no matter how low he got, he would still somehow rise to the occasion and paddle out.

Over the years, a lot of people – surfers and others – objected to the admiration and adulation, the cult of Dora ... on ethical and moral grounds. To be sure, Dora was a man of contradictions – unresolved and unresolvable, a mixed metaphor, a fractured and complex personality ... but with a core consciousness so solid and aware that no matter what the personalities did, he was almost always able to be true to himself. The proof is in the words: the stories he wrote, the stories he told, and the stories that will be told about him for a long, long time.

By October, he was sick and he knew it, but he wasn't letting on. Former Malibu surfer Bob Cooper, a life-long Latter Day Saint now living in Noosa Heads in Australia, got the picture right away. Flown in by event organizers for celebrity appearances at the annual surf festival in January of 2001, Miki didn't feel at all like socializing. When he went for a surf with Cooper, he had to stop to catch his breath on the trail to the beach, caught three waves during the session, and had a hard time making it back to the car with his surfboard.

"Was a waste of a life worth a few good waves and a legend?" Cooper wondered as Dora slipped out of sight.

Three months later, Miklos was in France, and Miki came to visit him in Bordeaux. "We had a lovely evening," Miklos remembered, "and Miki looked perfect! I have a picture of him, which was taken at the entrance of Chateau Lynch-Bages."

But in June he learned that his son had been diagnosed with cancer. "I can take care of it," Miki told him. "I told him to come home, we will get you a specialist, but Miki always knew everything better. He was very much against the establishment."

Dora tried various alternative practitioners (some would say charlatans) and was experiencing some success. His half-sister, Pauline, saw him in Paris in September and thought he looked fantastic.

But Harry Hodge, who watched over Miki in France, was concerned with what he was seeing, which was Miki starting to slip away. In California, Steve Pezman and Tom Adler put their heads together, got a lead on a promising new treatment. Prompted by his friends and a first-class ticket purchased by Harry, Dora decided to give it a try and flew home. Adler and Stecyk picked him up at the airport and drove him straight to Loma Linda hospital. All Dora wanted to do was talk about this book, to make sure it would happen. Even as the doctors hovered around him, assessing his condition, Miki went on about his book.

His doctor, Adrian Cotton found advanced pancreatic cancer, gave Miki a couple of months, and sent him home. Once there, friends began to arrive, the phone was always ringing, and Miki laid naked in the sun. Ceci came every day to massage him.

"Miki was very stoic," Miklos said. "I only saw him break down once, at home, in the last two months. In the first few weeks, he was still mobile – he went for walks, and he came and had breakfast. My wife Christine bought him every kind of juice you could imagine, but as the days passed by, he could eat less and less. And one day, at breakfast, he was sitting there, and he broke down. He couldn't eat anything, and he put his head down on the table, and he cried.

"'Everything was going so well for me for the last few years, and now it's finished.'

"And this was the only time. He had tumors in his throat, so he could not swallow. That's how Miki died – malnutrition. But the hospice was very good. They came to the house ... bathed him, cared for him, whatever he needed ... And then, of course, he was on morphine for the last two weeks."

On January 2nd, 2002, weakened and wretched but not witless, Miki joked to Greg Noll over the phone: "Well, they just gave me a shot of morphine and an enema. When I'm through with this conversation, I'm seriously considering doing a wall-painting."

Miki's favorite print burned in South Africa fire. Photo Le Roy Grannis

2001. Photo Taki

Before he hung up, Noll said, "Miki, I love you." And Miki answered, "Me too."

Miki Dora died the next morning, there in his father's house in Montecito. He asked that his ashes be spread along the San Ysidro trail in the mountains above Santa Barbara, where Miklos and Christine daily walk their dogs.

January 3, 2002. Out at Malibu. By the wall. Sun coming up. DORA LIVES! has again been spray-painted, in basic flat black, a dripping epitaph done minutes after he passed. The Los Angeles County Department of Beaches and Recreation graffiti abatement squad has not arrived to sandblast it off yet.

Spontaneous outbursts like this are still grafted onto lost tribal memories. As a result these statements are dutifully scrubbed from Rhoda Adamson's Marblehead-tile inlaid wall with the intent of leveling the playing field. The beach belongs to all of us. [Please deposit the appropriate amount in the appropriate slot marked with your parking spot number. Failure to do so will result in a citation, and your vehicle may be towed and impounded.]

Nearby, a man is sucking on warm stale ale recycled from the dregs of partially empty Newcastle Ale bottles left on the sand by last night's Pepperdine University revelers. The school team is called The Waves. This man is a local by inclination; he calls home a clump of coast prickly pear cactus around the point. He dispatches judgment on the sentiment expressed by urinating directly on the historic wall. Miki would have been partial to this eloquent act more than to any of the multitude of teary testimonials that were to follow. – CRS

The world is full of idiots, which is why I don't live there. – MSD

Written in 1988 in Bullhead, Arizona in a trailer owned by the sister of his girlfriend, Linda Cuy. Miki spent a solid month working on the piece, sometimes getting Linda's opinion on parts of it, carefully honing his first communication with the surfing world after more than 15 years of self-imposed exile. Dora was paid the highest sum in the history of *Surfer* magazine ($10,000) for the story, which was published in the July 1989 edition, following this introduction:

"Creator and prodigy of the Malibu Mystique, high-performance pioneer, standard bearer of the surf rebel, prophet of surfing's apocalypse and angry icon to an ever-expanding audience he unwittingly helped to create … Miki Dora has led a life dedicated to the ultimate free ride. Yet, in many ways, Dora has paid a high price for his philosophies of freedom: harassment and incarceration, gossip, notoriety and blatant commercial rip-offs have proved to be a relentless nemesis. He dropped off the public surf scene in 1974. Now, after years of wandering in the desert, both metaphorically and literally, Dora has delivered a new and ominously literal parable of our sport and our times."

MILLION DAYS TO DARKNESS
Death, Diamonds and the Episodic Wave
BY MIKI DORA

Without blurring the lines between fact and fiction and self-delusion, let me begin by recalling a few events.

The interrogation starts:

(Big Brother): Were you ever in the Military?

(Man in Custody): No.

Did you ever serve in any other Armed Forces?

No.

Did you ever work for the Government?

No.

Do you own any property?

No.

Do you have a home?

No – just Post Restante only.

Do you have any insurance or a pension?

No.

Do you have a bank account or credit card?

No.

Have you ever been on welfare or food stamps?

Nope.

Do you own anything?

Kenya. 1975. Photo Linda Cuy

No.

Have you ever been married?

Nope.

Are you homosexual?

Isn't everybody in this screwed-up country?

Who the hell do you think you are?

Who the hell do you want me to be?

Just answer the question, yes or no. How do you make your living?

By the oldest of livelihoods, Free Trade.

Now what the hell would that be?

Barter.

You're a liar! You're trafficking in drugs.

You owe the IRS $300,000. Case closed.

To quote Faustus: "Youth and debauchery are magnificent, but eventually you have the Devil to pay."

Stripped naked, I stood there manacled, shackled and chained, like any other slave caught in the 20th century, where human beings are trapped, brainwashed and otherwise destroyed by a mindless disciplinary process.

No Amnesty International or bogus Helsinki Accord.

With everything I owned confiscated, I was tossed a government-issue jumpsuit accompanied by the inevitable standard caustic remark, "Hey, man, what's your beef?" With one of my particularly favorite prosaic facade expressions, I responded,

"Among other things, improper abuse of credit."

A few of the local homeboys were checking me out as if I were a two-bit purse snatcher. One blurted out, "Oh, yeah, went to Vegas for the weekend, huh?" In my best diction, I replied, "No, not exactly. Just took a wee trip around world." "Huh? Oh, yeah! How long were you gone, man?"

And I was able to make the triumphant declaration: "Seven years, man!"

A loud cheer burst forth as the guard escorted me to my cell: Maximum Security, Terminal Island Federal Penitentiary, Long Beach, California.

From 1974 to 1981 I covered well over 200,000 miles over four continents 90% of the time reconnoitering the coastal areas of India, Africa, the Far East, Indonesia, Australia, New Zealand, South America and hundreds of islands.

Only in Europe did Interpol or the Feds ever get close. Only after five passports and millions of taxpayer dollars wasted on the hunt did I, with a gun pointed at my head, volunteer to return to the USA (just visiting, thanks), thus ending the most extraordinary surfing odyssey in the history of mankind.

Better to be judged by 12 than carried by six.

The way they laid down the law you'd have thought I was the top Burgermeister of the Baader-Meinhof, or that I was in the power of the Red Brigade, Black September and all their related modern counterparts.

In the course of time, with a stroke of the pen, I was finally kicked out of the pen with a federal misdemeanor, after being bottled up in their suffocating reform schools for two very long, solitary years.

It was all too absurd: no trial, no dark suit, no presidential pardon. They gave Nazi war criminals a better deal.

No doubt the question arises: Should I have gotten the firing squad for all those amazing escapades I pulled off during the fifties, sixties and seventies?

Anyhow, free again, I wasn't about to sit around waiting amid all the trappings of modern urban materialism and let TV rigor mortis infest my mind. I stand or fall, live or die, by my own decisions. To be splattered across a California freeway is not my idea of a rewarding end. I'll never rot in one of those jam-packed, clammy, dead-end cemeteries of the North. I'd rather be consumed by a Great White while riding perfect waves along the Wild Coast, or devoured by a desert lion while diamond gazing somewhere in the Namib, the oldest desert in existence, a land of splendor and grandeur, the land where man first walked this planet.

What better place to end one's life than in Primordial Africa?

By adopting my particular type of self-imposed exile I can outdistance these scourges of mankind: those who believe in consciousness without existence and those who believe in existence without consciousness—these caricatures who go to ludicrous lengths to assert their own importance, their own grotesque, overblown ambition.

The preconceived, hypocritical values of these scourges are their calling cards to the temples of mediocrity and cultural impoverishment. These schizos are forever in motion, spinning out of control, unable to slow down for fear someone might get a glimpse of their hollowness, their vulnerability and lack of moral courage, I wonder what the ancient Hawaiians would think of today's world. The once-prodigious, noble Hawaiian Enlightenment, with all its virtues, tribal loyalties and irrecoverable surfing skills, has in the end availed them nothing.

Africa represents a last chance for the Human Spirit; one of its few remaining opportunities to return to the place from whence it came.

Since most of you are not yet intimate with my idiopathic mind, let me explain that I've been commissioned by *Surfer* magazine to formulate my general principles of self-aggrandizement.

My hypothesis is $180°$ opposite to present-day logic (The Fool Plus One Theory), Quantum Waveriding being the prime factor in the equation.

As child prodigies sometimes do, I continue to discover my aptitude, which has endured to this present moment. If you are willing to accept the assertion that surfing is a colossal waste of time, then I'll concede I've wasted my life. But in a better and more graceful manner than any of my two-legged counterparts, no matter what the cost or consequences.

As manifested in today's environment, it is extremely more hazardous to compete with the five billion out-of-control human beings endlessly copulating and howling to the gods of growth and planned waste, rewarded with IOU paper promises to their nonexistent Promised Land.

I've been globe-trotting since the age of three months. Getaway is the name of the game, and I've been burning up the road ever since. The flames are in my blood permanently.
I grew up in probably the most perfect climate in the world. In that time dimension the California and Hawaii beaches were rarely used, mostly wild, untamed and breathtaking.

It's hard for me to believe, but at the time of Christ (that's not even one million days ago) there were only about 170 million people on Earth. For over 1,000 years, the world's population stayed about the same. Only near the turn of this century did the number of humans start to become troublesome. Then, with the introduction of the massive credit system, which gained momentum at the end of the fifties, unanimously endorsed by the economists, politicians, professors and forecasters, the population took off for the stratosphere.

Today, the world's population is out of control, raging like a prairie fire. When will the finite limits of the globe suffer a cataclysmic collision with a population gone wild? Will it take five, six or ten billion people? It is all the evolution of the human race relentlessly approaching its final destiny on this planet, a destiny which ultimately ignores the futile efforts of those who think they are shaping the world!

It's too awful for me to contemplate. When anthropologists look back on the sixties, seventies and eighties, they will shudder in disbelief.

"Let the fetus live so it can starve to death."

Undaunted, I'm going to continue to live and evolve in this irrational world, infected as it is with mysticism, superstition and grinding incompetence. The virus has spread to every aspect of life on our planet. Africa, in particular, is now riddled with demagogue dictators who make the megalomaniac Emperor Bukasa of the Central African Republic and Idi Amin look like pipsqueaks in comparison.

Reason and Justice are only mindless platitudes; the real rule on this planet is "Might is Right." You must either conquer and rule or lose and serve, triumph or suffer, be the hammer or the anvil. History gushes with blood.

The coup de grace was the Berlin Conference of 1878, which was bequeathed to Africa by the former Colonial Nations, cutting up the continent so these power brokers could plunder at will, eventually sapping the foundations of all tribal and linguistic uniqueness. It was a blow that will take generations to undo—if such a turnaround is even possible.

And the world wonders why the Black Continent is coming apart at the seams. Starvation in the hundreds-of-millions is inevitable. AIDS is pandemic. If a two-legged Black Mamba doesn't slit your throat, then a fervent patriot might just put a bullet between your eyes for blurting out liberal U.S. propaganda. The Afrikaners, Germans and British have no great historical compulsion to be unduly fond of one another; they act in desperate partnership here only because they realize that if they fail to hang together, they will hang separately.

Each day 375,000 black workers descend some 3,240 meters into the bowels of the Earth, to a depth at which temperatures increase by 1°C for every 50 meters of descent. These are the deepest gold mines in the world, and the richest.

The gold deposits of the Witwaterstrand are the greatest subterranean treasures so far found by man. Hundreds of black workers die every year through explosions, cave-ins, and so forth. Thousands of tons of rock and gravel are dug just to produce a few ounces of gold. Tons of the pure metal is shipped to Central Bank locations throughout the world, only to be placed underground, once again, in vaults.

The U.S. Government says this gold is worth only $42 an ounce, but anybody with a bit of common sense knows otherwise. The U.S. Government says gold is too valuable to be used as money. I presume then money should have no value.

It brings to mind that great American fanatic, William Jennings Bryan, who railed against crucifying mankind upon a Cross of Gold. Better to enslave him in a sea of debt.

It's a funny thing, in all the years I've lived in Africa (no affront intended to Irving Berlin) not once have I heard God Bless America sung. Unbelievable, eh? I keep my mouth shut, my mind alert, my eyes straight on riding a few extraordinary waves.

In 1970 Jeffreys Bay was still relatively unknown. It's been deteriorating ever since (like everyplace else). However, the real treasure chest of waves lies somewhere else. No matter what the population of the world ejaculates into, nobody is going to venture into this world within a world, wherein the Final Destination is the ultimate solitude – madness or death.

South of the Tropic of Capricorn, north of the meridian of the Cape of Good Hope, 30° south, 18° east…In the Heavens of the Southern Cross…below the sinister cycle of survival by killing and the endless sacrifice of the weaker in order in make the strong stronger: There lies Namaqualand and, north, the timeless prehistoric Africa, a world of primitive drives and desires, inhabited by the Gikwe-Bushmen 25,000 years ago during the Middle Stone Age. Their ancestors occupied the same territory continuously for 25 million years, since the dawn of the world, when Man and Beast were brothers. They are the oldest sitting tenants on Earth.

Near the mouth of the Orange River lay the richest deposits of gem diamonds in the world. They were probably washed down by prehistoric rivers from volcanic deposits inland. This soft material, known as "kimberlite" or "blue ground," is a rich alluvial stew, the most prized ingredient of which is the diamond.

In the language of the Hottentots, the word Namib, literally translated, means Waterless Land of Death. The Atlantic shore of Namib is known as the Skeleton Coast, a narrow belt of wasteland some 80-180 kilometers wide and more than 2,000 kilometers long.

The Skeleton Coast begins near the Olifants River in the south and ends near Mossameda in Angola to the north. Geologists blink their eyes and scratch their heads in disbelief when they first view the Namib. For myself, this is the most extraordinary geographical, biological, phantasmagorical piece of real estate I have ever come across. Bewildering and mesmerizing is this science fiction landscape, and vain is my attempt to explain or justify it. Suffice that it is one of the most savage and primeval scenes imaginable – almost incomprehensible to modern man.

Few things have changed here over the last few million years. Where great four-tusked elephants once made their own laws, roving bands of black-backed jackals have now inherited this living nightmare. Dwarf trees survive here that live 1,000 years, and have tentacle-like leaves which produce a flower every 25 years. This is the hideout of the baboon spider and the deadly black scorpion – and their number-one enemy, the golden mole, a ferocious predator. Like a surrealistic airbrushing, a few dust devils spin unconstrained over glistening, bright-yellow sand dunes. These dunes look like they've taken over the entire Earth, creating a mirage of unimaginable proportions.

The shoreline topography is a junkyard of rusting history littered with relics of old and modern shipwrecks, interspersed with whale skeletons, fossils, and semi-precious stones. Sporadically, washed-up corpses of giant squid – predator to the sperm whales that roam off the continental shelf in the cold South Atlantic depths – seem to levitate over the hot sands. Their ghostlike, distorted cadavers somehow reflect into the misty environment, encasing the sea and its waves, just a few meters away, in a shroud of ominous adversity.

Far above, in the metallic African atmosphere, a black eagle winding down on a current of air produces a very unsettling sensation.

This neck of land would make an impression on the most invincible of minds.

The Theory of Probability rapidly works against you the deeper you manage to penetrate into this surreal stretch of coastline, until the on-and-off chance of getting out alive becomes zilch.

Standing to the right, sand dunes higher than those of the Sahara or the Gobi play tricks with your sense of time. They were in existence 200 million years before the pharaohs. In this dry air your dehydrated body, too, would be perfectly preserved like the Egyptian mummies, forever, into perpetuity.

Ever seen a man dying of thirst? Do you know what happens to him? He lurches around in a tight circle, eyeballs bulging out of his head, choking, his tongue hanging down farther than his chin… cracked and swollen, like a chunk of rotting liver.

At this stage, it's a hundred-to-one shot he's going to kick the bucket.

Water gushing forth from subterranean artesian wells encircled by a lush date-palm oasis is simply a pipe dream.

Checking out the snakebite outfit and a couple of extra boxes of cartridges for the .375 Magnum Express, my Bushman sidekick and bodyguard makes our base camp only a quarter of the way in. The Land Rover contains our entire water supply. It would be a worthless piece of junk if anything major went wrong with it. Water is our most precious possession, and radiator evaporation wastes too much.

Nature here does not yield her secrets willingly. That's where my Bushman colleague comes in. His world is a very strange and ancient one. There is no doubt that the psychic powers of his people have remained more delicately tuned than ours. Keeping others alive and fed is his expertise. Do you think anything in this domain cares a hoot about Apartheid or Capitalism or Socialism or Religion or Man's Greed and Cruelties? This land remains totally indifferent to all human pretensions.

I would take only a Bushman on this venture; he can be trusted. A white man would freak out, drink all your water, put a bullet in your back, and nobody would be the wiser.

It is no traveler's tale or stretch of the truth when I say over five million carats of diamonds were recovered along these ancient beaches over a 15-year period, making the legendary King Solomon's Mines seem puny in comparison. Unlike those mined in the Transvaal, these are formed by volcanic action under the sea, and there are still millions more to unearth. The world-renowned, 128-carat Tiffany Diamond was found along this very coast.

However, my passion for great waves overshadows my lust for diamonds. If you think these are the sun stroked deliriums of a paranoid, let me try to explain. Just as when a negative is placed into a solution a faint image emerges, then only later in the process does the full picture become clear, so only in retrospect will this narrative become discernible, bringing the full picture into focus.

The average fathead would shrug them off as inconsequential specks of glorified glass. Perhaps. It's all in the way you perceive things. Have any of you ever held and turned in your fingertips a 20-carat, blue-white diamond, the purest and most sought-after stone of all? I think not. If you had, you would know you were holding a mysterious, compelling substance.

Do you have any idea of its worth? If I told you half, you'd call me a liar.

Its fiery beauty is as hard to account for as is its origin in the volcanoes that turned night to day in the Proterozoic Period. They are splinters of a mirror that simmered a hundred million years ago. In their blue-white heart is the broken image of our Earth as it existed at its birth. When you hold this gemstone you're holding a fragment of the basic element of our planet.

Alas, the unquenchable allure of kleptomania is always present. No one is immune. Lekker lewe: the sweet life or humbugged! Take my word for it: If you are not a master of brilliant cunning, don't even let it cross your mind. Let them lie where they are. You could lose your life. Many a man has.

In South Africa it's an offense against the State if you are caught with an uncut stone. The Golden Rule: If you find a diamond, throw it away.

A few years back this Australian bloke had a harebrained scheme to sailboard in, make his fortune, then sail up near the Angolan border. I warned him it would be a dangerous exercise in futility. He was sure he had all the answers, though, including the best escape route.

All brawn and no brain, puffed-up and arrogant, in full regalia he sailed off into the fog and resigned himself to Fate… never to be seen again.

A week-or-so later, near my encampment, I spotted a wandering Strandloper landing south. The origin of these Strandlopers is completely unknown. Even the Bushmen, who are conscious of everything, are confused about their aboriginal ancestry. There are only about a dozen Strandlopers left in existence. This naked anthrpoid was wearing the Australian's shredded boardshorts as his headdress.

It's been said before: "He laughs best who laughs last."
So, can one get out alive with his inheritance? It's highly unlikely. First off, walking out is a Herculean task. You probably wouldn't last the day. The Namib Desert is merciless.

To the south is the forbidden area of Consolidated Diamond Mines, De Beers and the Central Selling Organization. They make the law of the land, and their Diamond Detectives are harsh enforcers.

If you're arrested, expect to be held incommunicado, fluoroscoped, your hands tied into enormous metal-type gloves, then force-fed ample doses of laxatives. God help you if any diamonds are found. These chaps are humorless, slow-thinking and insufferably self-righteous.

There is no such thing as live-and-let-live in the diamond business. I know what I'm talking about. I've been through it all.

So … to the north, Angola and the ANC. If they catch you, a necklace party is guaranteed. I was once stopped by some Cuban commandos who were going to waste me on the spot. One guy understood a little French. I convinced him I was a French porno photographer and gave him the address of my worst enemy in Paris. I got their attention by promising that after they won the war I would give them all positions as stunt thespians in my next production. I ripped out a few sample pages from my outlawed, smuggled-in Penthouse mag as a teaser. They looked disarranged as I made a hasty retreat and got the hell out of there.

Of course, there's always the South Atlantic, but here we're dealing with unimaginable actualities. For some 5,000 kilometers southward from the Cape of Good Hope there is no other land, no shipping or trade routes, no aircraft, no weather stations, nothing. There is only the raging intensity of water whipped by the howling storms of the Roaring Forties. Circulating anticlockwise, the Benguela Current sweeps northward from Antarctica then collides with the warm Agulhas Stream and the Mozambique Current, causing massive ocean turbulences, generating chaos along the continental shelf and inducing a Maelstrom Effect. This provokes a frightening instability within the Coriolis Force.

One of the offshoots of these submerged disturbances is the Upwelling Principle, and one of the main danger zones is between the Walvis Ridge and the Cape Basin, where the real impending menace looms as Episodic Waves.

From all my investigations, I am convinced the luxury liner Waratah was hit by one of these rogue waves and lost without a trace in 1909 with 211 aboard.

According to my calculations, these killer waves are most likely to occur during the Vernal Equinox. For example, the *Mamohus*, a 93,000-ton tanker whose bows were swept away by one of these huge waves in 1966, miraculously survived the encounter. Most ships are not so fortunate; they are taken to the icy bottom in a matter of seconds.

Lloyds of London makes reference to the existence of these rogue monsters in its marine-indemnity policies as "the Episodic Wave Phenomenon." An encounter usually means a total loss and pay-out.

Annually, supertankers carry some 600 million tons of crude oil around the southern coast of Africa, bound from the Middle East for Europe and the Americas. If these sea routes were ever cut by the Russkies, Europe would freeze to death instantly and America's economy would probably cave in.

The way I figured it, the deeper I managed to get in with drinking water, the better the chances of getting back out alive. For this elementary reason I buried a few canteens at marked spots along the way, so that when I retraced my footsore steps I'd have an ample supply to prolong survival.

Alongside this strand of sand, always within a stone's throw, is an array of world-class point breaks.

This one: Out of the vast bed of South Atlantic Ocean there emerges, like a flash of greased lightning, a symmetrically smooth, 8' jet-black wall of water, spiraling over a craggy and jagged cluster of fossilized reefs. From its rooster-tail blow-back, its silvery rainbow spray glimmers, then vanishes into an inky, vaporous mist. It is a sight that would confound any observer.

Imagine a devastating, 100-yard, coiling stand-up cylinder breaking in 4' of water over a razor-sharp, crustacean-covered bottom. A split-second, vertical, semi-blind take-off must be executed with brute force for serious follow-through drive. Compulsory is maximum acceleration…and a full-out super trim.

One miscalculation and you're a dead man, being carried out of this world. Injured-only is impossible.

That's why equipment must be perfectly balanced. Bottom curve, rocker and rails have all been handcrafted from years of enlightened theory (by the eye only). No power tools are ever used. This understanding produces a heart-and-soul, 8'2" x 17-$^1\!/_2$"-wide, drawn-to-the-limit, classic single-fin pin.

Rest assured, in this domain each wave envelops and lambastes all five senses, leaving a lasting impression indelibly stamped in the subconscious. Two billion brain cells are inflamed, stimulating maximum concentration, computerized in Life-or-Death thrill ride that is unsurpassable, making everything else in life, by comparison, second-rate.

A day's walk farther north lies a panorama more deplorably desolate than human imagination can conceive, created by a seismic cataclysm a hundred million years ago. Here, I gaze at a sight no white man has ever seen.

From my vantage point: the scorched-dry river terrace of an ancient estuary. I can survey the ceaselessly heaving and churning undercurrents and the savage shorebreak. Beyond, an apparition – an optical illusion it seems at first, between the horizon and the shoreline – rising from the depths: an immeasurably huge, writhing, expanding wall of water. Its center looks like a hooded cobra head, swaying and heaving; its reflection, magnified on the gray-black, lacquer-smooth water below, exaggerates this abnormal monstrosity for a fraction of a moment, then it explodes into oblivion.

My sense of wonder is heightened and renewed by this deadly attraction. Lost in thought, I wonder if I have the courage. Existing on Bushman rice (insect larvae, ants and their eggs), chomping on other organic delicacies (snakes, scorpions, rats, mice, lizards, frogs and locusts), jacked-up on a protein high, gnawing on my last chunk of biltong, I am inspired by the gravity of this remarkable spectacle. Unhinged, yet curious to confront this hybrid, I am halted by a cautionary rush of adrenaline. There are very few events left in life that are free from Social, Political and Religious connotations, and this is unequivocally one of them.

Being sucked out through the rip was the easy part. Under the circumstances, the channel seemed safe enough – no erratic sets. In fact, 200 yards out, and nothing.

Going alone really doesn't rattle my nervous system that

much; I've been doing this my entire life, in hundreds of bizarre spots throughout the world.

But this experience was unique.

First off, the water seemed to stick to my fingertips, making it an effort to paddle with any speed. This was a bit unnerving. Then, without warning, it happened: In close proximity, a huge bubble erupted up out of the water. Within it appeared a gigantic, blunt head, then a body in airborne suspension, three times the size of a bull elephant, scaring the holy brownie out of me. I almost swallowed my tongue in a coronary fright.

Wrapped around the immense head, flailing spasmodically, were two tentacle-sucking arms and eight shorter ones. Then came the shrill, ear-splitting sounds of a giant cephalopoda squid getting munched, its black ink gushing and squirting like a broken fire hydrant, bits and pieces of flesh flying everywhere.

The battle lasted a few minutes. Then, with one gargantuan gulp, the sperm whale swallowed the whole goddamn thing. The 30', 400-pound body – all this nourishment consumed before my eyes – went down the whale's gullet in slow motion.

An enormous bloodshot eye gave me a quick once-over, but bubbling away in its digestive juices like a saintly Jonah was not to be my inexorable fate.

Temporarily disoriented, I found myself dead-center of an advancing set of waves. I barely made it over the second one, punching through the feathering mass.

Awestruck, unable to believe my senses, the third was a towering peak, pyramode in shape, unimaginable in size. I began to hyperventilate for my inevitable keelhauling, stroking for my life toward the channel and a last chance for escape.

Now, with an unnatural hissing sound … bending … this tremendous substance began to change its course, aiming straight for me. I knew in the back of my mind that I had survived closed-out Waimea, but this perpendicular, midnight-black wall of water with a Cyclopean center core was something else altogether.

Now the colossus was on me. With all my strength I paddled straight for the eye, then rolled and jabbed my stiletto through the very top. At that precise second the sun broke through the hazy atmosphere, illuminating the puncture I was coming through with thousands of dazzling, iridescent water particles. In the next instant everything was caving in.

I took my last gasp of air as the top third of this giant wave pitched out, tore my true love from my hands and snapped the legrope. In this fraction of a second, clinging like a spider to its web in a monsoon, looking back over my shoulder through this translucent skylight, I could see my board spinning out of control far beneath me.

Grabbing my knees in an egg-survival position, I anticipated a launch into eternity. During the plummet, I just missed cannonballing through the deck of my board. Fortunately, my back only glanced off the rail as the cascade of water above caught up with me. I tried desperately to thrash through the back, but it was not to be. The water held me tight, like a fly in a gluepot. The next moment was one of tumultuous, disjointed dispersion.

With most high-quality waves over 10', the exploding water is projected shoreward. In this instance, just the opposite occurred. The massive throw-out curved back into its own base, exploded inward and upward, forming a wave within a wave, theoretically devouring itself. Anyone caught in this Episodic Creation would be unmercifully spun in a horizontal vortex and plunged down to the icy depths for a soundless inspection of Davy Jones' locker. The secrets of all my triumphs are never to panic, and impeccable timing.

This Epilogue is not just entertainment, it is Real Life. To thoroughly end my account of this experience would take at least 20 more pages. Highly impractical, Labor lost. Superfluous to the limited attention span of this magazine's frivolous fraternity.

In short, tucked away in a safe deposit box in Paris are all the photographs, sketches, charts and maps of the expedition, including a 10-carat black diamond encased in a fossilized oyster shell. In addition, there is my exhaustive data, collected over a 20-year period, on the explanatory premises of the Episodic Wave Theory. Conceivably, someday I shall finish this accounting verbally, over a bottle of Mouton '45, with an individual who has a highly inquisitive mind. Until that very hour the bourgeoisie must be reconciled to their customary Orwellian entanglements, rushing to be saved by technology … and then saved from it.

In the words of Confucius: "Bloodhound who keep nose too close to ground never see charging tiger."

Yellow Banks. 1968. Photo Brad Barrett

1933 Miklos Kornel Dora and Ramona Stanclif meet in Vienna. He is a Hungarian law student and officer in the Royal Calvary. She is a 17-year-old American on tour with her mother.

1934 Miklos Sandor Dora is born in Budapest, Hungary on August 11.

1935 In January, the couple and infant son arrive in Los Angeles; Miklos begins work as a sales representative for Hungarian wineries.

1935-7 They live with Stanclif in-laws at 1551 Murray Dr. in Silver Lake District of L.A.

1937 Miklos establishes the "Little Hungary" restaurant on Sunset Blvd.

1937 Miklos' mother, Nadina DeSanctis, arrives in L.A., helps raise Miki.

1937-9 Family moves to Larrabe Street in West Hollywood.

1938 First surfing trip to Palos Verdes Cove with Miklos.

1939 Miklos takes Miki on several camping trips to San Onofre.

1939 Ramona meets Gard Chapin through her sister Juanita.

1939 Ramona and Miklos divorce, Miklos moves to Westwood.

1939 Miki attends St. John Military Academy.

1940 Briefly attends boarding school in Perris, California.

1940 Enrolled in UES in L.A.; renowned for its progressive approach.

1942 Lives with Madam DeSanctis in West Hollywood.

1945 Builds surfboards with Gard Chapin and Bob Simmons in the latter's workshop on Riverside Dr., North Hollywood. Dora later asserts Chapin's classified knowledge led to his death.

1946 Chapin gives him Lindsay Lord's treatise, *The Naval Architecture of Planing Hulls*. He is tutored on hydrodynamics and wave forms by oceanographer Dr. Walter H. Munk, husband to one of his Gard's sisters, who attended Cal Tech with Bob Simmons. The informal group of Chapin-Simmons-Munk-Lord-Dora undertook the first systematic modern study of surfboard shape and construction.

1948 Miklos Sr. sells Little Hungary and moves to Argentina, goes into the shrimping business off Mar Del Plata.

1948-52 Attends Hollywood High School.

1950 Using salvage balsa, Dora takes eight months to build his first surfboard in Madam DeSanctis' garage. He drills out the board's core and inserts ping pong balls in the voids in hopes of creating a lighter, more responsive craft.

1950 Hitches ride to Rincon to test-ride new board, loses it on his initial paddle out in a large west swell, swims ashore to find beach covered with bits of balsa and ping pong balls.

1951 Bill Bridgeman, a surfer and a social acquaintance of Chapin and Miki, pilots a Douglas D-558-ll Skyrocket to Mach 1.88.

1952 Visits Haiti on the way to Argentina to visit his father.

1952 Surfs Chile and Peru on return to US from Argentina.

1952 Registers for draft but is rejected due to lifelong asthma condition.

1952 Begins surfing regularly at Malibu Point.

1953 Joe Quigg sells his Malibu "easy rider" to Chapin for Miki. A revolutionary, highly-influential craft, Dora considered it his "greatest board,"

1953 Caught stowing away on a cruise ship to Hawaii, Miki and friends are arrested outside the two-mile limit, held in custody, and jailed in Honolulu on arrival. Dora alone pleads not guilty.

1954 As guest of C. E. Allen Barnard (director of materials procurement),

Miki shops freely for fiberglass, resin, aluminum, and plastics at Douglas Aircraft's company salvage store.

1954 Simmons drowns in big surf at Windansea off La Jolla on Sept. 24.

1955 Works as parking attendant at the new Beverly Hilton Hotel.

1955 Hosts at Frascati Restaurant on Wilshire Blvd.

1955 Miklos returns to Los Angeles from South America.

1956 Employed by prominent L.A. wine distributor, the Alfred Hart Co.

1956-7 Gard Chapin disappears in Baja.

1957 Obtains his first polyurethane-foam-cored surfboard, built in Santa Monica by Dave Sweet, the first manufacturer using this revolutionary technology. While troubled, the Dora-Sweet relationship spans decades; Miki often obtaining Dave's foam blanks via clandestine intermediaries.

1957 Jack Kerouac's novel, *On the Road*, is published.

1957 *Gidget, the Little Girl with Big Ideas* by Frederick Kohner is published by G.P. Putnam's Sons (New York), and some actions by Miki Dora are acknowledged as being the basis for key activities in the book.

1959 Doubles lead James Darren as Moondoggie in the Columbia Pictures film of *Gidget*.

1959 Dora frequents the Scarab sports-car factory on 1042 Princeton Dr. in Venice, where he shares owner Lance Reventlow's passion for powerful, quick-handling cars. Reventlow's engines were rumored to be the key to Dora's formidable record of victories on the Mulholland Dr. underground racing circuit.

1959 Miki regularly visits the Velzy and Jacobs surfboard shop, also located in Venice at 4821 Pacific Ave.

1959 Miki runs over JFK as he body surfs at State Beach.

1959 The third stop in Dora's Venetian triad is the Gas House (1501 Ocean Front Walk), the coffeehouse/performance space occupying the building that housed the Mecca Buffet in the heyday of Abbot Kinney's Pleasure Pier. Here Miki congregated with beat artists, poets, musicians, writers, and luminaries like Wallace Berman, Edmund Teske, Tex Kleen, Eric "Big Daddy" Nord, John "Cooksy" Thomas, Duke Herd, Ken Strickfaden, and John Haag. Dora wheeled and dealed surfboards, wine, rare books, automobiles, and speed racing parts, functioning as go-between among A, B, and C list celebrities and the counterculture.

1960 John Severson publishes the *"First Annual Surf Photo Book,"* titled *The Surfer*, a slim magazine sold to patrons of his new film, *Surf Fever*. This turns out to be the first issue of *Surfer* magazine.

1961 Phil Hill becomes the first American to win the World Driving Championship. During his Santa Monica youth, Hill and Topanga Beach resident Bobby Talmadge had built a number of souped-up autos favored by the surf set, including Chapin, Joe Quigg, and Bruce Brown.

1961 Pilots a 7'11" Dale Velzy foam board that is 24" wide.

1961 Performs in *Gidget* sequel, *Gidget Goes Hawaiian*, meeting actor Wally Cox via the surf-prop provisioner. The two socialize periodically with other self-proclaimed industry outsiders, including Arthur Lake II, Keenan Wynn, Marlon Brando, Brook Hudson, and Stan Laurel.

1962 In Tahiti at time Brando is involved in filming of *Mutiny on the Bounty*.

1962 Excluded from first Malibu Surfing Association Club Invitational contest, as he belongs to no club.

1962 Attends Andy Warhol's first soup-can paintings exhibit at Ferus Gallery on La Cienega, where he is aware of artists like Kenny Price, Billy Al Bengston, and Robert Irwin from contacts on the beach.

1963 President John F. Kennedy is assassinated in Dallas on Nov. 22. Dora is troubled by this event, having met JFK through fellow waver-rider Peter Lawford, and becomes obsessed with Kennedy's killing.

1963 Joins Windansea Surf Club, and MSA members loudly complain that Dora is a ringer for the future Malibu interclub contest.

1963 Featured in magazine ads as a team rider for Jacobs Surfboards (Hermosa Beach). Owner Hap Jacobs observed that, "with Dora, you never knew if he was riding the boards or selling them."

1963 Miki has a small role in the Universal release of *King of the Mountain*, which stars Marlon Brando, Shirley Jones, and David Niven.

1963 Appears in *Beach Party*.

1964 Doubles Bobby Vinton as the lead in *Surf Party*. Dora's surfing image is used as the iconic logo of the film, and, in one version, Vinton's oversized blanched face is crudely pasted onto Dora's decidedly darker body. Miki's dreams are subsequently haunted by the *Surf Party* tag line:"When beach boys meet surf sweeties – it's a real swingin' splash of fun, fun, fun!"

1964 *Muscle Beach Party* reveals Miki surfing, stunting, and acting; he is shown dancing on the theater poster.

1964 General Motors Corp. begins sales of the new Chevrolet Malibu.

1964 Malibu Ltd. sponsors Dora to an Australian Surf Shop board built by Bob Cooper and Tom Morey. The stick features Morey's interchangeable polypropylene skeg system (TRAF), which allows Miki to modify fins and immediately see the effects. He appears in a Malibu Ltd. ad in Surfguide,

posing in front of Chasen's Restaurant.

1964 The third annual MSA Club Invitational contest is televised by KHJ-TV. Commentators Bob Feigel and Stan Richards speculate on Dora's self-defeating motive for riding a 12-foot tandem board in the semifinals.

1964 Portrays a college student in *For Those Who Think Young* and a surf bum in *Bikini Beach*.

1964 Gary Weiss as "Sunny Oceans" releases hit single *I'm her lover man*.

1964 Appears opposite Gene Barry in TV drama *Burke's Law*, episode "Who Killed the Surf Broad?"

1964 Shaves chest and doubles Fabian Forte in *Ride the Wild Surf*, shot on location on the North Shore of Oahu. Plays ski bum in *Ski Party*; publicity photos depict Dora on slopes in alpine attire alongside bikini-clad ingénue Patti Chandler.

1964 Miklos Dora, Sr. becomes associate of Rothschild wines.

1965 Coaches Sally Field in the art of surfing for the TV incarnation of *Gidget*. Field is the daughter of legendary stuntman Jock O'Mahoney, former Palos Verdes lifeguard and friend of Chapin. The actress' half brother is the surfer-photographer James O'Mahoney, who frequently crossed paths with Dora over the years.

1965 Dora instigates aggressive tactics in the finals of the Malibu Invitational; Johnny Fain is the target. Promoters of the sport are embarrassed. Miki throws away his trophy at the awards ceremony.

1965 Tests Reynolds Yater's prototype Spoon surfboard.

1965 Appears in characteristically redundant sand saga, *How to Stuff a Wild Bikini*. Bonds with Buster Keaton, who was a friend of Chapin a quarter of a century earlier when the actor lived at Topanga Beach.

1965 Greg Noll Surfboards releases Da Cat signature model surfboard in Manhattan Beach. Da Cat features an extreme scooped nose and raked flexible fin.

1965 Invitee to the inaugural Duke Kahanamoku Surfing Championships at Sunset Beach in Hawaii.

1965 Inducted into the International Surfing Hall of Fame at a ceremony at Santa Monica Civic Auditorium.

1966 Visits a West Los Angeles garage, which is home to John Martin's Black Sparrow Press and buys a book of poems by Charles Bukowski.

1966 Longtime friend Phil Edwards is shown alongside swimsuit models holding unwaxed Hobie Surfboards in an illuminated 18' x 60' Kodak Colorama billboard on a wall of New York's Grand Central Station.

1966 Publishers of *Surfer* and *Surfing* magazines admonish Greg Noll for "negative content" in Da Cat ads. Nevertheless, the ads run.

1967 Executes a proper "BA" in front of the judges stand at the MSA contest.

1967 Greg Noll Surfboards releases Da Cat 2 series, which has a removable higher-aspect-ratio ABS fin, twin slot flutes in the board's rear planing section and a more blended spoon nose. This incarnation also is offered in a pintail configuration.

1967-8 Miki winters at a North Shore compound with a varying cast of associates, including Michael Hynson, Russell Hughes, Melinda Meriwether, David Nuuhiwa, Bunker Spreckels, and Herbie Fletcher.

1967 Rents assorted surfboards to Ricky Nelson's TV show, *Malibu U.*

1967 Appears in film *The Sweet Ride* starring Jacqueline Bisset and Tony Franciosca. Surfing crew is sequestered at Point Conception, where,

through the beneficence of Herbert Edison Fletcher, Dora comes across a 9'2" Harbour Sol Model, sculpted by Michael "Red" Marshall.

1968 Visits the Broad Beach, Malibu home of Richard "Papa" Ellis, where Elvis Presley is coincidentally filming *Live a Little, Love a Little*.

1968 Da Cat 2 mini-boards are released. These models are similar to the '67 version but are ridden a foot or two shorter.

1968 Bing Copeland and David Nuuhiwa present Dora with an 8'6" Dick Brewer-shaped Lotus pintail board.

1968 Robert F. Kennedy is assassinated by Sirhan B. Sirhan at a Democratic Party reception by the Coconut Grove in the Ambassador Hotel on Wilshire Blvd. Miki Dora, who is present at the affair, is questioned by authorities; his detainment and interrogation is initially reported in Deke Keasbey's "Surf Line" gossip column in the *Santa Monica Evening Outlook*.

1968 Miki co-designs (via an intermediary) a stringerless, flexible-resin-coated 7'11" board through Dave Sweet. The board is created without a conventional fiberglass-and-resin shell and is extremely light, flexible, and maneuverable.

1968 Travels to France, later meets Miklos and the two travel on to Hungary to visit Miki's birthplace.

1968 Richard Nixon is elected POTUS.

1968 Dora threatens to sue Santa Monica surfboard maker Rich Wilken for listing him as a team rider in an Wilken Surfboard ad in *Surfer* magazine.

1969 Heavy rains reduce Santa Monica State Beach and Malibu (Miki's preferred local surf spots) to beachbreak slop for the foreseeable future.

1969 Bunker Spreckels (sugar heir and Clark Gable's stepson) shapes a 6'6" hard-edge round-tail slab board for Miki.

1969 Acts in the Karen Valentine feature *Gidget Grows Up*. Dora's delivery of the plot-advancement, line, "Hey gang, Gidget's back!" is most certainly tinged with heartfelt irony.

1969 In California, rides Yater "Pocket Rocket" with textured deck on giant winter swells. He is somewhat back in Renny Yater's good graces following a shared winter hiatus at Honolua Bay on Maui.

1969 Speaks with Bill Bahne, Michael Hynson and David Nuuhiwa about appearing in *Rainbow Bridge* documentary with Jimi Hendrix on Maui, but ultimately passes on the opportunity.

1970 Travels to Brazil, Paraguay, Uruguay, Argentina, and the Caribbean in scam adventure organized by Malibu surfer Don Wilson along with buddies Alan Carter and Greg "Mongoose" Meisenholder. In Rio, attends Governor's Ball with Bob Beadle and bounces a $50,000 check for jewels.

1970 An impromptu visit to *Surfer* magazine publisher John Severson's home at Cotton's Point elicits a heavy-handed search of Dora's car and person by Secret Service agents. Severson's house is directly adjacent to the Western White House. Miki is convinced that John's sale of photographs he took of the Nixons to Life magazine has alienated the powers that be.

1970 Release of *Pacific Vibrations*, a film by John Severson, which includes a pithy Dora interview and animated shots of him in the film's title sequence.

1971-5 Travels Europe with (alternately) Linda Cuy and Marcia McMartin.

1971 To Guethary, France in August with Marcia McMartin.

1971 Back to California, travels to Baja.

1973 Visiting former world surfing champion Nat Young. Miki buys skiing equipment at Mammoth Lakes, California. Agrees to back up his guest's purchase and unwittingly writes out a bad check. He is arrested on April 3 and charged with felony fraud.

1973 Winter hike into Kalalau Valley on Kauai's north shore with Joey Cabell and Denny Aaberg. High tide entrapment freaks Miki, who carves a huge SOS in the sand hoping to summon helicopter rescue. Later Miki connects with Bunker, also on Kauai.

1973 Travels: Costa Rica, London, Columbia, Panama and return to US.

1974 Fails to appear and post bail as ordered; subsequently, changes his plea four times, finally pleading guilty on Sept. 27. Gets three years of probation and a $1,500 fine, also is prohibited from possessing credit cards, required to have a job and an "approved" residence, plus must check in regularly with parole officer.

1974 Nixon resigns the presidency.

1975 On April 11, Court issues warrant for Miki's arrest for probation violation; bail is set at $10k.

1975 Travels to Switzerland, London, Austria, Australia, Greece, Egypt, Turkey, Lebanon, India, Ceylon, and ends up at Gisborne in New Zealand, where possessions shipped ahead from California have been seized on the dock by authorities.

1975 Miki and Linda aquire Epinor and Rognon, King Charles Spaniels.

1976 Leaves New Zealand, travels to Australia, Mauritius, Kenya, and Europe (Alps, Spain, Italy, and Portugal)

1976 Camps in van alongside Kempton's Biarritz farmhouse for 8 months.

1976-7 Travels throughout Spain, Portugal, Italy, and Morocco.

1976-7 French Alps, Chamonix, Lesarc, w/Yves Bessas and Rick Peterson.

1977 Spends March and April in the Canary Islands.

1978 Escapes from U.S. Embassy in Milan after trying to secure new passport.

1981 Arrested by French authorities making illegal phone calls from pay phone; serves three months in Bayonne jail.

1981 Flies first-class back to California in Sept., met at LAX by FBI agents.

1982 July 22nd, Denver, federal grand jury sentences Miki to 6 months.

1982 Serves time at Bridgeport in Mono County and Lompoc in California. Released from Lompoc federal prison on Dec. 17th.

1983 Returns to Europe, lives in France in the green van, golfs in Ireland, back to Calif. to pick up a Bruce Jones board in Seal Beach in April.

1983 Exploratory trip to South Africa and Jeffreys Bay.

1983 With receipt of court-ordered restitution ($4,456 paid by Miklos, Sr.) in August, Mono County issues a waiver to Miki, allowing him to leave country.

1983 Despite his efforts to prevent it, *California* magazine publishes, "*The Legend Lives*," a profile of Dora by David Rensin in the August issue.

1984 Diners Club triggers the forced sale of Dora's possessions by Barwick's Auction House in Gisbourne, New Zealand. The Malibu Phantom and Mickey the Maori buy and return a few personal mementos.

1984 Aquires Scooter Boy – a King Charles Cavalier Spaniel – in Ireland.

1986 Moves to Jeffreys Bay, South Africa.

1989 Visits France.

1990 Visits California and is interviewed by Bill Delaney for his in film the *Surfers*. Herbie Fletcher shoots additional footage in Baja.

1993 Dora v. Frontline Video. Case heard in California's 4th Appellate Court, in which plaintiff Dora brings suit against producer of surfing documentary, *The Legends of Malibu*, seeking damages for the unauthorized use of his name, voice, and likeness. Court determines Miki is a public figure performing a public act in a public place and therefore not entitled to compensation. Case often cited subsequently as setting precedent.

1995 Los Angeles County Sheriff deputies arrest a man charged with making bogus Da Cat surfboards and selling them to unknowing collectors. Upon viewing the counterfeits, Greg Noll comments, " The guy was a pretty good craftsman; in the old days I would have given him a job."

1995 Lives and surfs in South Africa.

1996 Noll and Miki re-release the Da Cat model as the most expensive limited edition surfboard to date. It becomes an enormous success.

1996 Unauthorized documentary *In Search of da Cat* is produced in England by former Malibu surf rider Andrew Salazar.

1998 In June, fire destroys his rented flat overlooking Supertubes at Jefferies Bay; loses papers and possessions, but most tragically, Scooter Boy dies in the fire.

1999 Tours Cuba, surfs its eastern coast. In Habana, meets Alberto Korda.

2001 Travels to Chile with Chris Malloy.

2001 Lives next to Hotel Madrid in Guethary, returns "home" for last time.

2002 January 3 – Miklos Sandor Dora dies in Montecito, California.

This book is dedicated to Miki's family: Christine, Miklos and Pauline Dora

Acknowledgements. Laura and Greg Noll (who initiated this project over ten years ago), Harry Hodge (Miki's generous and protective friend), Steve Pezman, Robert Simpson, Mike Murphy, Chris Rohloff (whose father's footage became a key part of the project), LeRoy Grannis, Stephanie and Dewey Nicks, Joe Quigg, Alice and Peter Gowland, Brad Barrett, Steve Taussig (who first brought Miki by my studio in the late '80s to discuss this book), Pat Darrin, Jim Fitzpatrick, Rick Hodgson, Matt Warshaw, Linda Cuy, Ceci Clouse, Rick Peterson, Bob Feigel, Phil Jarrett, Yves Bessas, Susan Kampion, Bill Hasley, Bill Delaney, Melanie Berry, Frank Boros, Allan Carter, Greg Meisenholder, Dr. Adrian Cotton, Charlie Exxon, Jim Mellor, Nat Young, Mickey Muñoz, Bob Beadle, Bob Cooper, Derek Hynd, Scott Hulet, John Millius, Denny Aaberg, Ray Kunze, Sonny Miller, Michael Halsband, Frank Curtis, Steve Gilbar, Phil and Trudi, Susan McKnell (Surf Hut), Eric Chauche, Laurent Miramon, Martin Sugarman, Tim Bowler, Paul Gross, Randy Hild, John Bathurst, Danny Kwock, Bob McKnight, Jim Kempton, Richard Slade, Sally and Rennie Yater, Jim O'Mahoney, Dan, Keith & Chris Malloy, Hans Hagen, Mark Oblow, Santa Barbara Hospice, Rick Grigg, George Downing, Jeff Hakman, Taki, Prosper Keating, Richard Buckley, Joey Cabell, Peaches, Mark Cunningham, Mark Fragale, Robert and Matt Tomaszewski, Jean Charles Caze, Dominic Taylor, Sally Field, Jennifer Rima, Gary Weiss, Kathy Kohner, Frank Donahue, Toni Donovan, Mark Renneker, Don James Estate, Art Brewer, Barrett Tester, Steve Jones, Jim Heimann, Fred Hemmings Jr., Maritxu Darrigrand, Linda Burnham and Robert Overby, Jeff Divine, Dale Velzy, Gary Lynch, John Elwell, Surfer magazine, Steven Baker, Doug Wood, Dan Emmett, Virginie Miramon, Jeff Hornbaker, Fred Hild, Audrey, Luke, Alexis, Bill and Gail Adler, Jamie Budge, Marcia McMartin, Jacquie Allen, George Diskant, Austin Reiter, Lee Kaplan, Matt Kivlin, G.T., John Levin, Tak Matsuda, Carrie Simpson, Bobby Tan, Dale Hope, Graham and Laura Peake, Ron Stoner Estate, Donna Wingate, Avery Lozada, Elisa Leshowitz, James Danziger, Ariel Meyerowitz, Jodi Beck, James Gilbert, David Fahey, Joe Howell, Kurt Wahlner, John Balkwell, Sandra Reese, Kelly Slater, Mary Randolph Carter, Lee Norwood, Spencer Birch, Dave Kalama, Titus Kinimaka, Ann Lam, Danny Abromovitz, Hugh Milstein, David and Peter at Integrated Communications, Mandy Martin, Philippe Lauga, Dash Rosenberger, NI Syndication LTD, Joe Dugan, David Rensin, Billy Edwards, Duke Howard, Buffalo Keaulana, Rusty Miller, Strider Wasilewski, Karen Shapiro, Stacy Peralta, Cristiana Janssen, Maria Barnes.